Garden Appliqué

Terrece Beesley & Trice Boerens

Martingale
& COMPANY

Bothell, Washington

Garden Appliqué
© 1999 by Terrece Beesley and Trice Boerens

Martingale & Company
PO Box 118
Bothell, WA 98041-0118 USA
www.patchwork.com

Printed in Hong Kong
04 03 02 01 00 99   6 5 4 3 2 1

That Patchwork Place is an imprint
of Martingale & Company.

Credits

President . . . . Nancy J. Martin
CEO/Publisher. . . . . Daniel J. Martin
Associate Publisher . . . . Jane Hamada
Editorial Director . . . . Mary V. Green
Design and Production Manager . . . . Cheryl Stevenson
Editor . . . . Margaret Shields Marti
Technical Editor . . . . Dawn M. Anderson
Illustrator . . . . Cherie Hanson
Photographer . . . . Brent Kane
Artists . . . . Trice Boerens, Terrece Beesley

Library of Congress Cataloging-in-Publication Data

Boerens, Trice.
    Garden appliqué / Trice Boerens and Terrece Beesley.
        p.   cm.
    ISBN 1-56477-292-6
    1. Appliqué Patterns.   2. Patchwork Patterns.
    3. Quilting Patterns.   4. Gardens in art.
I. Beesley, Terrece.   II. Title.
TT779.B645 1999
746.44'5041—dc21   99-22867
                                                        CIP

MISSION STATEMENT

*We are dedicated to providing
quality products and service by working
together to inspire creativity and to
enrich the lives we touch.*

Table of Contents

INTRODUCTION—5

BASIC INSTRUCTIONS—7

    Preparing Your Project—7

    Appliquéing—7

    Constructing the Quilt—10

    Mitering Corners—10

    Quilting—11

    Signing Your Project—11

    Framing Your Design—11

    Embroidery Stitches—12

QUILT PROJECTS

    Flower Basket Pillow—16

    Flower Basket Quilt—20

    Seasonal Coasters—25

    Four Seasons Pillow—31

    Fruit Coasters—35

    Lemon and Orange Topiary

        Wall Hangings—38

    Mixed Fruit Topiary Wall Hanging—43

    Garden Place Mat and Napkin—50

    Teapot Wall Hanging—54

    Tea Wall Plaques—60

    Cat in the Garden Pillow—70

    Wreath Pillows—80

    Sunshine Wall Hanging—88

    Autumn Leaves Wall Hanging—98

    I Love My Garden Wall Hanging—106

    Sow Good Seeds Wall Hanging—116

ABOUT THE AUTHORS—128

Introduction

"What was paradise?
but a garden,
an orchard of trees
and herbs, full of
pleasure, and nothing
there but delights."

William Lawson

Our garden is the subject of this book. After all, gardens hold more colors and shapes and textures than we could ever think of on our own!

Fruit has a shelf life of about three days. Or does it? This book offers you a way to create beautiful arrangements of fruits and vegetables, and whimsical garden landscapes that will last forever. It is an inviting sampling of colorful appliqué projects designed to bring the outdoors in. We provide you with "seeds" of inspiration, along with clear photographs, comprehensive diagrams, detailed instructions, and easy-to-use appliqué patterns.

Because we love our gardens, we sought new ways to enjoy their universal appeal. Our experience is in turning bits and pieces into art, and giving our readers inventive designs and imaginative uses for them. Scraps of fabric and strands of floss are the "rakes and hoes" of our trade. We have employed technology to provide accurate patterns, replicating the fabric colors and shapes you will need to make your project every bit as delightful as ours. But feel free to experiment. A person's quilt should be as individual as her garden.

Emphasizing simple but sophisticated designs, this book is intended for the novice as well as the experienced quilter. The appliqué pieces in this book can be worked with either needle-turn or fusible appliqué techniques. Needle-turn appliqué is the kind of handwork your grandmother had in her lap on long summer afternoons. Her rhythmical, even stitches made it seem almost as though the design piece were being woven into the background. Fused appliqué is the contemporary technique your best friend used to decorate the tote she made you. Quite simply, paper-backed fusible web and a hot iron allow you to join two pieces of fabric without making a single stitch. Pretty easy!

A garden is a place of refuge. Our hope is that completing the projects in this book will bring you the same quiet sense of satisfaction we experienced in creating them.

Trice Boerens and Terrece Beesley

Basic Instructions

Preparing Your Project

Tightly woven, 100% cotton fabric is your best choice for quiltmaking. Yardages are based on 44"-wide fabrics with trimmed selvages, and they allow for shrinkage and differences in layout. Wash, dry, and press all fabrics before marking and cutting any pieces. All cutting measurements for pieced segments include ¼" seam allowances. Appliqué patterns do not include seam allowances; you will need to add those as you cut out the pieces. When the instructions call for scraps, the required pieces are smaller than a piece of typing paper. For anything larger, the instructions specify an amount.

Work with good scissors. Small, sharp scissors that cut to the point are a good choice both for cutting out small design pieces and for clipping. Rotary cutters are a wonderful aid for cutting blocks and strips.

Turn your imagination loose—the sky does not always have to be blue. When choosing fabric, don't limit yourself to solids and small-scale prints. A large-scale print might include just the splash of color you need for a tiny appliqué piece. If you've found the right shade but the print is too busy, consider using the "wrong" side. (Who's to say what's wrong and what's right in a quilt?)

Use fabrics that are tightly woven, especially for small pieces, because they will fray if the weave is loose and be more difficult to work with. When appliqué pieces overlap, select pieces that contrast. Follow the color key included with the patterns only to the extent that you like our combinations and have scraps that are similar. Branch out whenever you can.

Finish a few blocks or the pillow top before you buy fabric for sashing or borders. For quilts that will be framed, complete the entire quilt before selecting the frame or mat board. The border fabric or the frame and mat board should complement but not overpower or compete with the blocks. Take the quilt blocks with you and try them against several fabrics (or frames and mats).

Appliquéing

Appliqué should have smooth curves and sharp points. Practice and patience have long been recommended as the best tools. One of the pleasures of appliqué is working with the small fabric pieces, turning them one way or another to achieve a new effect. Even the most difficult pieces can be worked with a needle-turn method. Contemporary needleworkers have the option of using fusible appliqué, a technique which employs paper-backed fusible webbing. Both techniques are used in the projects in this book.

Needle-Turn Appliqué

Traditional appliqué is needle-turn appliqué, and the needle is the most important tool. Choose a long, fine needle, preferably a #11 or #12 Sharp, that feels good to you. Work with short lengths of fine cotton thread, and sew with one strand. If you can't match the color of the fabric exactly, a shade that's darker and duller will blend better than lighter and brighter. For a medium-value print with several colors, medium gray will blend well.

Needle-turn appliqué is simply turning under the seam allowance on a design piece and slipstitching it to the background fabric. Pin or baste the design pieces in place. You may wish to trace the patterns onto the background, using an air-soluble or water-soluble marker, to ensure correct positioning. As you plan the placement, note which pieces overlap others.

Use your needle to turn under the seam allowance 1" or 2" ahead of where you are stitching, creasing the fold line with your fingers. Slipstitch the appliqué to the background fabric, using tiny, even stitches about ⅛" apart on straight edges and even closer around inside curves and sharp points.

To make the edge lie flat on inside curves, clip the seam allowance almost to the fold line. Clip excess fabric from tips of corners to eliminate bulk. Inverted points, such as where the tree branches meet the tree trunk on the "Sow Good Seeds" quilt on page 116, call for special attention because they are subject to fraying. To prevent fraying, take smaller stitches as you near the inverted point, and make several overcast stitches at the point itself.

Fusible Appliqué

Begin by acquainting yourself with the properties of paper-backed fusible web. On the smooth side—the paper side—you can trace patterns using an ordinary pencil. On the rough side you can feel the crystals that melt when they come in contact with the heat of an iron.

All the patterns in this book face the right way; that is, the way they appear in the finished project. For fusible appliqué you need to transfer the patterns to the fusible web in reverse, as outlined in the following instructions, so that they will face the right way after fusing.

Preparing the Pattern Pieces

Trace the full pattern onto tracing paper, using a heavy pencil line. You will use this pattern twice—first as a template for tracing pieces onto fusible web, and later as an overlay to guide placement.

Turn the tracing-paper pattern face down. Place the fusible web, paper side up, over the pattern. Place both pieces over a light box or hold them up to a window, then retrace the pattern pieces individually onto the paper side of the fusible web. Trace pieces that are to be cut from the same fabric (such as all green leaves) in groups, allowing about ¼" between pieces. (The colors on the pattern pieces indicate which pieces to cut from the same fabric.) Cut the web in one piece, about ½" from the pencil lines. You are ready to fuse a piece or group of pieces to fabric.

Know your iron. A few experiments and you can tell how many seconds and what temperature settings give you the best results. It doesn't take long to fuse the web to the fabric, maybe two or three seconds. Fusing is like preparing pasta; you don't want to overcook it.

For each pattern piece and corresponding fabric, place the rough side of the web against the wrong side of the fabric. Fuse for two or three seconds until your pattern piece is fused to the fabric. At this point, your pattern piece is still backwards from the photo and from the pattern in the book.

Pin the tracing-paper overlay to the background fabric, along the top edge only. The pattern overlay will remain in place throughout the appliqué process.

Fusing the Pieces

Cut out the appliqué pieces along the pencil lines. When working with small pieces, it's best to cut only two or three at a time. Peel the paper backing from the web. Place the cut-out fabric piece right side up on the background, using the pattern overlay as your guide. Now the piece will correspond with the photo and the pattern. Fuse in place.

Continue to fuse a few pieces at a time, following the pattern overlay. When they have cooled, check to see that all the pieces are adhering well, especially at the edges.

- When working with solid colors, you may turn the web in any direction you want. In fact, variety in the grain positioning enhances the finished product. If the fabric pattern is important to the design, such as stripes in a border piece, plan carefully as you trace the pieces onto the web and fuse the web onto the fabric.

- In most cases when the instructions call for a print, the appliqué piece is small and does not contrast much with the background color; for example, the fabric may have small white leaves against a cream background. In some cases, the designated fabric color is uneven and when the small pieces are cut out, they appear to be from different fabrics. The variations add to the interest of the design.

- When the embroidered design on a project contains lettering or is more detailed than you wish to draw freehand, use a water-soluble or air-soluble marking pen or transfer pencil to draw placement lines. For any of the tools, follow the manufacturer's instructions and experiment before using it on a project. To use the transfer pencil, trace the lettering from the pattern in the book onto tracing paper, using a heavy pencil line. Then turn the pattern over. Trace the lettering using the transfer pencil; it will be backwards. Place the transfer pencil pattern right side up where you want it on the fabric. Iron.

Constructing the Quilt

To prepare two pieces for joining, place them right sides together, matching seams when appropriate and securing them with pins. Stitch with a ¼" seam, using about twelve stitches per inch. For best results, press seams as you go. Always press a seam before crossing it with another.

Mitering Corners

The diagonal lines of mitered corners add a crisp finish to borders and require only a little extra effort. To ensure perfect mitered corners, begin by folding each border strip widthwise to find its center. Mark the center with a pin. Also mark the center of each edge of the quilt top. With right sides together, match the center of the border to the center of the quilt top. Stitch the pieces together, starting and stopping ¼" from the corners; backstitch. Repeat the centering and stitching for each edge, allowing the border strips to hang loose.

Fold the right sides of two adjacent strips together and stitch a diagonal (45-degree) seam.

Open the border pieces to check your work. The diagonal seam and the two seams joining the borders to the quilt top should meet but not overlap. Trim the seam allowance on the diagonal seam to ¼". Repeat for each corner.

Quilting

Quilting stitches are used to secure the backing, batting, and quilt top together, often in a pattern that enhances the design. Quilting can be done either by hand or machine and with quilting thread that matches or contrasts.

Signing Your Project

Always sign and date your work. You can use a permanent pen or embroidery to mark your name and the date. Some quilters sign and date their work on a separate piece of fabric and slipstitch it to the back; others write or embroider on the quilt back itself. With either method, the information enriches the quilt.

Framing Your Design

Some of the appliquéd projects in this book have been framed by a professional framer for easy display. To set off your appliquéd artwork, choose a wood or metal frame that complements your design. You may also want to select a colored mat board that coordinates with the fabrics in your piece.

To frame your work, proceed with the following instructions to pad your design and stretch it over a mounting board. Then have a professional frame the design. If using a mat board, specify the size of the window opening and the desired width of the mat.

Materials

3/16" mounting board, such as foam-core board
Polyester fleece
Strong thread and needle
Acid-Free double-stick transfer tape for framing or acid-free mounting adhesive
Utility knife and ruler

1. Determine the area of the design that you want visible in the window opening of the frame or mat board. If using a mat board, determine the desired width of the mat.
2. Calculate the outside dimensions of the artwork or mat board. If using just a frame, this measurement is usually ½" larger than the window opening. If using a mat board, this measurement is usually equal to the dimensions of the mat board window opening, plus 2 times the width of the mat board plus ½". For example, if using a mat board with an 8" x 10" opening and a 1½" width, the finished outside dimension of the design and mat board would be 11½" x 13½".
3. Cut the mounting board slightly smaller than the outside dimensions of the artwork determined in step 2, using the utility knife and ruler. The mounting board should fit loosely onto the lip of the frame.
4. Cut a piece of fleece to the dimensions of the mounting board and secure it to the board with strips of double-stick transfer tape or acid-free mounting adhesive.
   Trim your artwork to 3" wider and longer than the mounting board. If your artwork is not large enough, stitch a strip of muslin to each side.
5. Place the mounting board, fleece side up, over your work surface; center the artwork over it. Pin the fabric to the edges of the board at the corners and centers, aligning the grain of the fabric with the edges of the board. Continue to stretch and pin the fabric to the sides of the board, spacing pins about ½" apart.

6. Fold the extra fabric to the back, folding in the excess at the corners and turning under the raw edges. Trim away some of the bulk at the corners, and stitch in place.

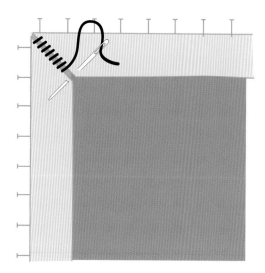

7. Lace the fabric edges from top to bottom, using a strong thread. Pull the lacing taut. Repeat lacing from side to side, pulling taut. Remove the pins.

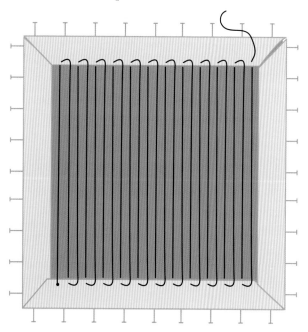

Embroidery Stitches

Backstitch

Bring the needle up at 1, down at 2, up at 3. Go back down at 1, and continue in this manner.

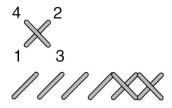

Cross Stitch

Each single cross is made of two stitches forming a cross. Large areas or rows may be worked by first stitching across the row from left to right. Complete the crosses by working back across the row from right to left. All top stitches should slant in the same direction.

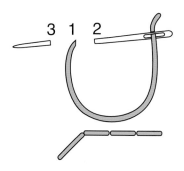

Buttonhole Stitch

This stitch is worked from left to right. Bring the thread out at 1. Insert the needle at 2, and bring it out at 3, stitching over the first stitch. Insert the needle at 4 and repeat.

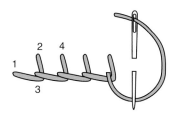

Chain Stitch

Bring the needle up at 1, hold down a small loop of thread, and insert the needle at 2. Bring the needle up at 3 and insert it at 4, guiding the needle over the loop and securing the previous loop with the loop just formed. Repeat, securing each loop with the next to form a chain. Take a small stitch over the end of the last loop to secure the end.

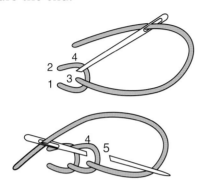

Couching

Use these simple stitches to anchor a length of floss or ribbon to fabric.

French Knot

Bring the needle up at 1 and wrap floss once (or twice) around the shaft of the needle. Insert the needle into the fabric at 2. Change the size of your knot by varying the strands used or wrapping more times.

Satin Stitch

Bring the needle up at 1 and down at 2. Repeat, making parallel stitches to fill an area.

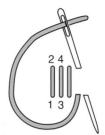

Stem Stitch

Bring the needle up at 1, down at 2, up at 3, and down at 4, keeping the thread to the left of the needle.

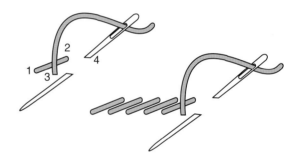

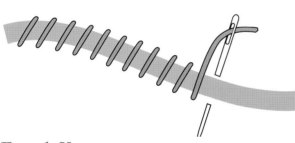

Quilt Projects

Flower Basket Pillow

Finished Size: 11" x 11"

Materials

Scraps of cotton fabrics in these colors:
bright blue print, tan print, burgundy print,
black/tan print, brown solid, and brown
stripe
7½" x 7½" piece of black/tan check
14" x 16" piece of light brown print for
corner pieces and backing
Thread to match fabrics
3" x 3" piece of paper-backed fusible web
Polyester fiberfill
Tracing paper and pencil
Air-soluble or water-soluble marking pen

Appliqué the Block

*Note: Refer to "Needle-Turn Appliqué" and "Fusible
Appliqué" on pages 8–10 for general instructions. Refer to the
project photo and pattern for placement.*

1. Trace the stems on page 19 individually
   onto tracing paper.
2. Trace the stems onto fusible web, then cut
   them out ½" from the marked lines. Fuse
   the stems to the wrong side of the bright
   blue print scrap.
3. Trace the basket and flower patterns onto
   tracing paper, adding ¼" seam allowances.
   Referring to the photo and color key, pin the
   patterns to the corresponding fabrics and
   cut on the outer marked lines.
4. Fold the black/tan square into quarters and
   mark the center. Cut out the bright blue
   stems on the marked lines. Peel off the
   paper backing and place the stems on the
   black/tan square, fusible side down, placing
   the lower edge of the center stem just over
   the center mark on the block. Fuse the stems
   to the block.
5. Using needle-turn appliqué, stitch the basket to the square, then the 3 flowers. Trim
   the square to 6½" x 6½".

Piece the Pillow Top

1. From the brown/black print, cut 4 strips,
   each 1¼" x 6½".
2. From the brown solid, cut 4 strips, each 1¾"
   x 6½".
3. From the brown stripe, cut 4 strips, each
   1¼" x 6½".
4. From the light brown print, cut 4 squares,
   each 3¼" x 3¼".
5. To make the pieced border strips, sew
   together 1 brown/black, 1 brown solid, and
   1 brown stripe piece, using ¼" seam
   allowances. Repeat with the remaining
   pieces to make 4 pieced border strips.

Make 4

6. Sew 1 light brown square to each end of a
   pieced strip, aligning the edges and using a
   ¼" seam allowance. Repeat with a second
   pieced strip. Set aside.

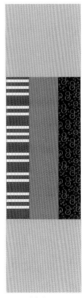

Make 2

7. Sew pieced border strips to the top and bottom of the appliqué block.

8. Sew the 2 remaining pieced borders to the sides of the block, aligning seams.

9. From the light brown print, cut an 11½" x 11½" square for the pillow back.

10. Using a ¼" seam allowance, stitch the pillow front and back right sides together, leaving an opening on 1 edge. Stuff firmly with fiberfill. Slipstitch the opening closed.

Flower Basket Pillow Pattern

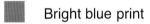 Bright blue print

Tan print

Burgundy print

Flower Basket Quilt

Finished Size: 30½" x 30½"

Materials

Scraps of cotton fabric in these colors: bright blue print and burgundy print

⅜ yard of 44"-wide tan print for baskets

¾ yard of 44"-wide black/tan check for blocks

¼ yard of 44"-wide navy/black print for triangle corners

1 yard of 44"-wide light brown print for sashing and border

1 yard of 44"-wide dark brown print for backing

1 yard of 44"-wide polyester fleece

8" x 12" piece of charcoal felt for sashing squares

Thread to match fabrics

White embroidery floss

¼ yard of paper-backed fusible web

Tracing paper and pencil

Air-soluble or water-soluble marking pen

Appliqué the Blocks

Note: Refer to "Needle-Turn Appliqué" and "Fusible Appliqué" on pages 8–10 for general instructions. Refer to the project photo and pattern for appliqué placement.

1. Trace stems for 16 blocks onto fusible web, then cut them out ½" from the marked lines. Fuse the stems to the wrong side of the bright blue print scrap.

2. Trace the flower and basket patterns (page 23) onto tracing paper, adding ¼" seam allowances. Referring to the photo and color key, pin the patterns to the corresponding fabrics and cut on the outer marked lines. Cut 48 flowers and 16 baskets.

3. From the black/tan check, cut 16 squares, each 7½" x 7½". Using the corner triangle pattern on page 24, cut 64 triangles from the navy/black print. The blocks and triangles are oversized and will be trimmed to fit the quilt dimensions later.

4. Fold a black/tan check square into quarters and mark the center. Cut out the stems for 1 block. Peel off the paper backing and lay the stems on the background, fusible side down, placing the lower edge of the center stem just over the center mark on the block. Fuse the stems to the block.

5. Stitch the basket to the block using needle-turn appliqué, then appliqué 3 burgundy flowers in place.

6. Repeat steps 4 and 5 to complete 16 blocks.

7. Using 2 strands of white embroidery floss, make 1 French knot (page 13) in the center of each flower.

8. Trace the trimming template on page 24 onto tracing paper. Place the template over the right side of a block, aligning the outline on the template with the basket and the outside edges with the grain line. Trace around the edge of the template. Sew 1 triangle to each corner of the block, right sides together, using the marked line as the seam line. Press the triangles flat. Trim the block to 6½" x 6½". Repeat to attach triangles to all the blocks.

Piece the Quilt Top

1. From the light brown print, cut 12 sashing pieces, each 1½" x 6½"; 3 sashing pieces, each 1½" x 27½", and 4 border pieces, each 2¾" x 44".

2. Sew 1½" x 6½" sashing pieces to the right-hand edges of 12 blocks, using ¼" seams.

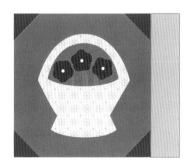

Make 12

3. Sew 3 blocks with sashing together and 1 block without sashing into a row. Repeat to make 4 rows.

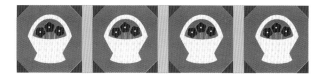

4. Sew the 1½" x 27½" sashing pieces to the lower edges of 3 rows. Join the rows, adding the fourth row of blocks.

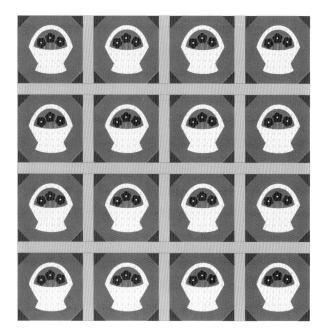

5. Add the border strips, following the instructions for "Mitering Corners" on pages 10–11. Press the quilt top. Cut a piece of dark brown print the same size as the quilt top. Cut a piece of fleece the same size as the quilt top.

6. Lay the fleece on your work surface, then place the backing and quilt top over it, right sides together. Stitch ¼" from the edges, leaving an opening in 1 edge. Cut the fleece from the seam allowance and trim the corners. Turn the quilt right side out and slip-stitch the opening closed. Press the edges.

7. From the felt, cut 25 squares, each 1¼" x 1¼". Beginning in the center of the quilt and working outward, pin felt squares at the intersections of the sashing strips. Sew an X through the middle of each square. Pin and stitch the border squares in place, placing 1 square at the end of each sashing strip and 1 at each corner.

Flower Basket Quilt Pattern

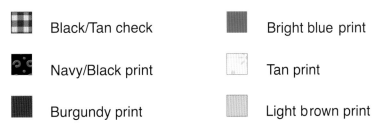 Black/Tan check		Bright blue print	
Navy/Black print		Tan print	
Burgundy print		Light brown print	

Flower Basket Quilt Pattern

Corner triangle

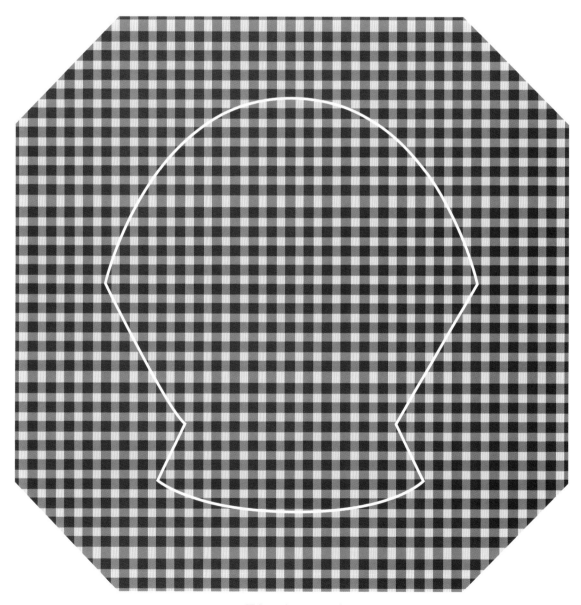

Trimming template

Seasonal Coasters

Finished Size: 5¼" x 5¼"

Materials

All Coasters
White thread
Scraps of fusible web
Tracing paper and pencil

Individual Coasters

One Spring Coaster
Scrap of dark pink felt for backing (outer border)
Scrap of blue-green felt for inner border
Scraps of cotton fabric in these colors: gold, green check, green print, rose, tan print, navy blue, purple, and orange check
Embroidery floss in these colors: gold, navy blue, and brown

One Summer Coaster
Scrap of dark pink felt for backing (outer border)
Scrap of white felt for inner border
Scraps of cotton fabric in these colors: lavender, navy blue, green, and gold
Embroidery floss in these colors: navy blue, brown, white, and medium blue

One Fall Coaster
Scrap of blue-green felt for backing (outer border)
Scrap of white felt for inner border
Scraps of cotton fabric in these colors: light green, brown, and rust print
Embroidery floss in these colors: medium brown and rust

One Winter Coaster
Scrap of blue-green felt for backing (outer border)
Scrap of white felt for inner border
Scraps of cotton fabric in these colors: blue print, navy blue, and white
Embroidery floss in these colors: navy blue and light blue

Make the Background

1. Trace the coaster backing pattern on page 30 onto tracing paper. Cut out the pattern on the drawn line and pin it to the felt for the backing. Cut around the edge of the pattern.
2. Cut a 4⅛" square from the felt for the inner border. Center the square over the backing. Stitch with white thread very close to the edge of the inner border square.

Appliqué the Design

Note: Refer to "Fusible Appliqué" on pages 8–10 for general instructions. Refer to the project photo and pattern for appliqué placement.

1. Using the desired pattern on pages 28–29, cut the accent rectangle used behind the motif from a scrap. Cut a 4" square from a scrap for the background, using the project photo as a color reference. Using 1 strand of embroidery floss, sew the accent rectangle to the background square with a running stitch. Use gold floss for the spring coaster, navy blue floss for the summer and winter coasters, and brown floss for the fall coaster.
2. Using the desired pattern, make a pattern overlay for the coaster (pages 8–9).

3. Draw a 4" square on fusible web, then use the overlay to trace all the remaining pattern pieces onto the web.

4. Fuse the background square to the center of the felt inner border piece. Pin the overlay to the background and leave it in place throughout the appliqué process.

 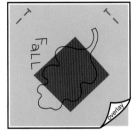

5. Trim the web ½" from the drawn lines. Fuse the pieces to the wrong sides of the corresponding fabrics. Complete the appliqué for each coaster as follows:

Spring Coaster

Trim fabric pieces for the large butterfly on the marked lines. Peel off the paper backing and place the green print wings on the background, fusible side down, using the overlay as a guide to placement. Fuse the wings in place. Cut out and fuse the rose wings, then the tan print wings and navy blue body. For the small butterfly, cut out and fuse the purple wings, then the orange check wings and navy blue body. Remove the overlay.

Summer Coaster

Trim fabric pieces for the flower on the marked lines. Peel off the paper backing and place the green stem on the background, fusible side down, using the overlay as a guide to placement. Fuse the stem in place. Cut out and fuse the gold petals, then the green flower center. Remove the overlay.

Fall Coaster

Trim the fabric piece for the leaf on the marked line. Peel off the paper backing and place the leaf on the background, fusible side down, using the overlay as a guide to placement. Fuse the leaf in place. Remove the overlay.

Winter Coaster

Trim the fabric piece for the snowflake on the marked line. Peel off the paper backing and place the snowflake on the background, fusible side down, using the overlay as a guide to placement. Fuse the snowflake in place. Remove the overlay.

Embroider the Details

Note: Refer to "Embroidery Stitches" on pages 12–13 for stitch diagrams. Refer to the project photo and patterns for placement.

Spring Coaster

Using 2 strands of navy floss, stem-stitch the antennae. Using 2 strands of brown floss, stem-stitch the lettering.

Summer Coaster

Using 2 strands of brown floss, make long stitches that radiate from the flower center. Using 2 strands of white floss, make a French knot in the center of the flower. Using 2 strands of medium blue floss, stem-stitch the lettering.

Fall Coaster

Using 2 strands of brown floss, make large running stitches down the middle of the leaf. Using 2 strands of rust floss, make 7 French knots on the stem. Using 2 strands of rust floss, stem-stitch the lettering.

Winter Coaster

Using 2 strands of light blue floss, satin-stitch the 3 small circles outside the snowflake. Using 2 strands of light blue floss, stem-stitch the lettering.

Navy blue

Gold

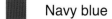 White

Rose

Tan print

Orange check

Green

Purple

Green check

Rust print

Green

Brown

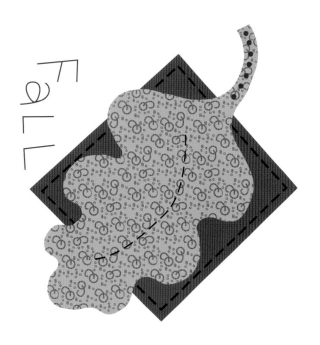

Coaster backing

Four Seasons Pillow

Finished Size: 11¼" x 11¼"

Materials

Scraps of cotton fabric in these colors: blue
print, gold, lavender, light green, navy blue,
green check, brown, green print, rose, tan
print, purple, orange check, green, rust
print, and white

⅛ yard of 44"-wide navy blue fabric for outer
border

4" x 9" piece of light blue print for inner
border

11½" x 11½" piece of navy print for back

Thread to match fabrics

Embroidery floss in these colors: navy blue, gold,
brown, light blue, medium blue, and rust

⅛ yard of paper-backed fusible web

Tracing paper and pencil

Air-soluble or water-soluble marking pen

Polyester fiberfill

Appliqué the Design

Note: Refer to "Fusible Appliqué" on pages 8–10 for general instructions. Refer to the project photo and patterns for appliqué placement.

1. Cut a 4½" x 4½" square from each fabric: blue print, gold, lavender, and light green.
2. Using the patterns on pages 28–29, make a pattern overlay for each block (pages 8–9) as shown in diagram 1 below. Use the pattern overlay to trace all pattern pieces except the accent rectangles onto the fusible web. When all the pieces have been traced, pin the overlays to the squares and leave them in place throughout the appliqué process.
3. Using the patterns on pages 28–29, cut out the following accent rectangles: 2 navy blue, 1 green check, and 1 brown. Baste the rectangles to the blocks, stitching ⅛" from the raw edges. Stitch the navy rectangles with 1 strand of navy embroidery floss. Use gold floss on the green check rectangle and brown floss on the brown rectangle. Use the pattern overlay as a placement guide (diagram 2).

Diagram 1

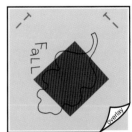

Diagram 2

4. Cut ½" from the drawn lines on the web. Fuse the pieces to the corresponding fabrics.

5. For the spring block, trim fabric pieces for the large butterfly on the marked lines. Peel off the paper backing and place the green print wings on the background, fusible side down, using the overlay as a guide to placement. Fuse the wings in place. Cut out and fuse the rose wings, then the tan print wings and navy blue body. For the small butterfly, cut out and fuse the purple wings, then the orange check wings and navy blue body. Remove the overlay.

6. For the summer block, trim fabric pieces for the flower on the marked lines. Peel off the paper backing and place the green stem on the background, fusible side down, using the overlay as a guide to placement. Fuse the stem in place. Cut out and fuse the gold petals, then the green flower center. Remove the overlay.

7. For the fall block, trim the fabric piece for the leaf on the marked line. Peel off the paper backing and place the leaf on the background, fusible side down, using the overlay as a guide to placement. Fuse the leaf in place. Remove the overlay.

8. For the winter block, trim the fabric piece for the snowflake on the marked line. Peel off the paper backing and place the snowflake on the background, fusible side down, using the overlay as a guide to placement. Fuse the snowflake in place. Remove the overlay.

Embroider the Design

Note: Refer to "Embroidery Stitches" on pages 12–13 for stitch diagrams. Refer to the project photo and patterns for placement.

1. For the spring block, use 2 strands of navy blue floss to stem-stitch the antennae. Use 2 strands of brown floss to stem-stitch the lettering.

2. For the summer block, use 2 strands of brown floss to make long stitches that radiate from the flower center. Use 2 strands of light blue floss to make a French knot in the center of the flower. Use 2 strands of medium blue floss to stem-stitch the lettering.

3. For the fall block, use 2 strands of brown floss to make large running stitches down the middle of the leaf. Use 2 strands of rust floss to make 7 French knots on the stem. Use 2 strands of rust floss to stem-stitch the lettering.

4. For the winter block, use 2 strands of light blue floss to satin-stitch the 3 circles outside the snowflake. Use 2 strands of light blue floss to stem-stitch the lettering.

Make the Pillow

1. Join 2 blocks, using ¼" seam allowances, then join the remaining pair. Sew the pairs together. Press.
2. From the light blue print, cut 4 strips, each 1" x 9". Align a strip with the edge of the pieced unit, right sides together. Stitch the strip to the unit, stopping 2" from the end of the strip.

3. Open the border strip, finger pressing the seam allowances toward the border. Working counterclockwise, stitch the next 2 strips to the unit, stitching to the ends.

4. Add the last strip. Return to the first strip and stitch the last 2". Press.
5. From the navy blue fabric, cut 4 strips, each 1¾" x 10½". Stitch them to the pillow top as you did the light blue strips.
6. Place the pillow top and 11½" navy blue print square right sides together, aligning edges. Stitch the 2 pieces together using a ¼" seam allowance and leaving an opening along one edge for turning and stuffing. Trim the corners and turn. Stuff firmly with fiberfill. Slipstitch the opening closed.

Fruit Coasters

Finished Size: 4¾" x 4¾"

Materials for One Coaster

5" x 10" piece of blue felt
Scraps of cotton fabric in these colors: light green, green check, lavender, gold, orange, red print, and purple
7" x 7" piece of blue/green print
Embroidery floss in these colors: brown and blue
Scraps of fusible web
Tracing paper and pencil
Air-soluble or water-soluble marking pen

Appliqué the Design

Note: Refer to "Fusible Appliqué" on pages 8–10 for general instructions. Refer to the project photo and pattern for placement.

1. Cut the blue felt into 2 pieces, each 5" x 5".
2. Using the pattern on page 37, make a pattern overlay for the design, including the blue felt background.
3. Use the pattern overlay to trace the fruit and leaf pieces onto fusible web. Pin the overlay to a blue felt square and leave it in place throughout the appliqué process.
4. Cut ½" from the drawn lines on the web. Fuse the pieces to the wrong sides of the corresponding fabrics.
5. Cut out the lavender plums on the drawn line. Peel off the paper backing and place the plums on the background, fusible side down, using the pattern overlay as a guide. Fuse the plums to the background.
6. Following the numerical sequence, cut out and fuse the remaining pieces of the design, except for the 2 grapes, which will be fused to the background later.

Embroider the Design

Note: Refer to "Embroidery Stitches" on pages 12–13 for stitch diagrams. Refer to the project photo and pattern for placement.

Using 2 strands of brown embroidery floss, buttonhole-stitch around the apple. Chain-stitch the apple and pear stems. Make 3 French knots on the orange.

Finish the Coaster

1. Apply fusible web to the wrong side of the blue/green print. Peel off the paper backing. Center the remaining blue felt square on the wrong side of the blue/green print. Trim the corners of the blue/green print as shown.

2. Fold 2 opposite edges over the felt; fuse. Fold and fuse the remaining edges.
3. Cut out the blue felt background. Center it on the coaster front. Using 2 strands of blue floss, sew running stitches ⅛" inside the edges of the appliquéd square, securing it to the coaster base. Leave the felt unstitched around the leaves on the lower left and around the plums and apple on the right side of the coaster.
4. Fuse the 2 remaining grapes in place.

Fruit Coasters Pattern

Lemon and *Orange*

Lemon Topiary Wall Hanging

Topiary Wall Hanging

Orange Topiary Wall Hanging

Finished Size: 7½" x 9½"

Materials for One Wall Hanging

11" x 10" piece of brown/black print
11" x 3½" piece of navy print
Embroidery floss in these colors: gold and brown
11" x 13" piece of polyester fleece
Tracing paper and pencil
Air-soluble or water-soluble marking pen
For lemon topiary—Scraps of cotton fabric in these colors: gold, yellow print, green solid, green print, tan solid, and tan print
For orange topiary—Scraps of cotton fabric in these colors: orange solid, orange print, green solid, green print, tan solid, and tan print

Make the Background

Stitch the brown/black and navy prints together along the long edges.

Appliqué the Design

Note: Refer to "Needle-Turn Appliqué" on page 8 for general instructions. Refer to the project photos and patterns for appliqué placement.

1. Trace the desired pattern (page 41 or 42) onto tracing paper, adding ¼" seam allowances. Referring to the photo and color key, pin the patterns to the corresponding fabrics and cut on the outer marked lines.
2. Mark the trunk placement onto the background. Appliqué the tan solid trunks in place.
3. Appliqué the tan print pot over the lower ends of the trunks.

4. Complete the appliqué in the following order: Lemon—appliqué the solid green leaves, green print leaves, gold lemons, and then the yellow-print lemon. Orange—appliqué the top green print leaf, orange-solid oranges, remaining leaves, and then the orange-print orange.

Embroider the Details

Note: Refer to "Embroidery Stitches" on pages 12–13 for stitch diagrams. Refer to the project photos and patterns for placement.

1. For each topiary, use 2 strands of gold floss to chain-stitch the thin trunk.
2. For the lemon topiary, use 2 strands of brown floss to stitch 7 French knots on the yellow-print lemon. For the orange topiary, use 2 stands of brown floss to stitch 6 French knots on the orange-print orange.

Frame the Design

Note: Refer to "Framing Your Design" on pages 11–12 for general instructions.

Have a professional framer frame the piece, padding it with the fleece.

Lemon Topiary Wall Hanging

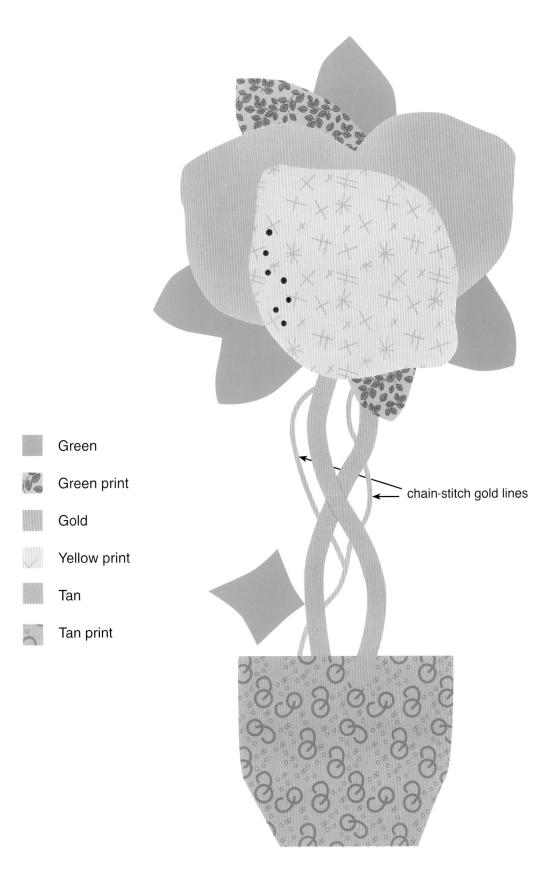

Green

Green print

Gold

Yellow print

Tan

Tan print

chain-stitch gold lines

Orange Topiary Wall Hanging

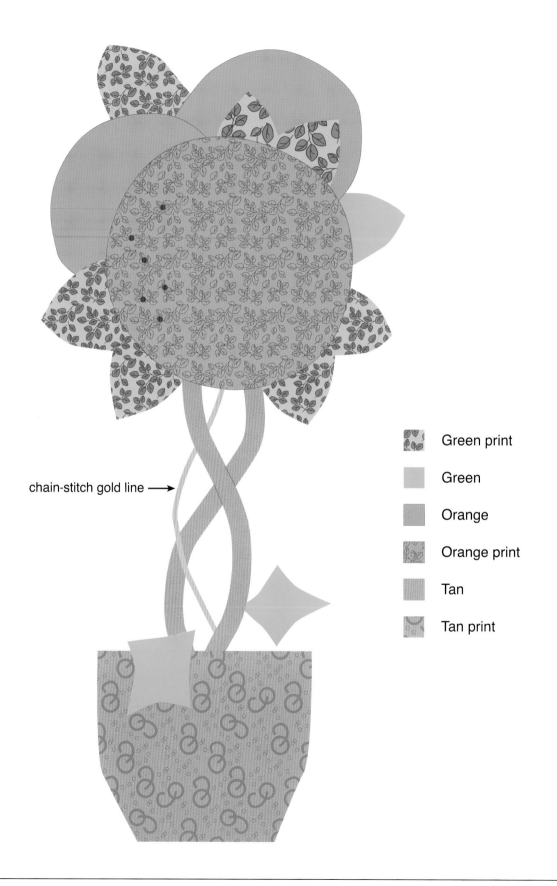

chain-stitch gold line →

Green print

Green

Orange

Orange print

Tan

Tan print

Mixed Fruit Topiary Wall Hanging

Finished Size: 11½" x 15½"

Materials

Scraps of cotton fabric in these colors: navy blue, turquoise print, brown/black print, gold print, dark gold print, orange print, red print, rose, lavender, blue, green check, green print, dark green, light green, tan solid, and tan print

15" x 19" piece of blue-green print for background

Embroidery floss in these colors: light green, dark green, rust, brown, pink, and purple

15" x 19" piece of polyester fleece

Tracing paper and pencil

Air-soluble or water-soluble marking pen

Make the Background

1. From navy blue fabric, cut 7 strips, each 4½" long, varying the widths between 1½" and 1". Appliqué the strips to the lower edge of the background fabric as shown, leaving 3" on each side.

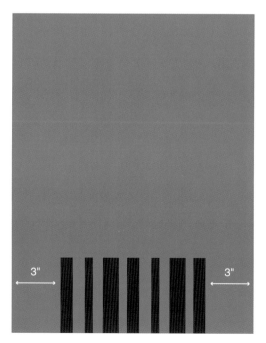

2. Cut a 1½" x 15" strip from the turquoise print. Appliqué the strip horizontally over the ends of the navy strips, 4¼" from the lower edge.

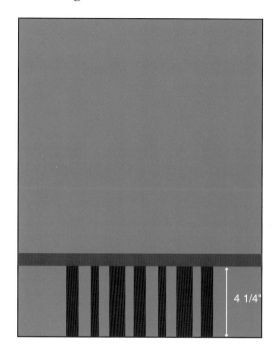

3. Join arch patterns A and B on pages 48 and 49 along the dashed lines. Cut the arch from the brown/black print. Appliqué the arch, centering it horizontally on the background, ¼" above the turquoise print strip.

Appliqué the Design

Note: Refer to "Needle-Turn Appliqué" on page 8 for general instructions. Refer to the project photo and pattern for appliqué placement.

1. Trace the pattern pieces (pages 46–47) onto tracing paper, adding ¼" seam allowances. Referring to the photo and color key, pin the patterns to the corresponding fabrics and cut on the outer marked lines.
2. Mark the placement of the trunks on the background. Appliqué them in place.
3. Appliqué the pot at the base of the trunks.

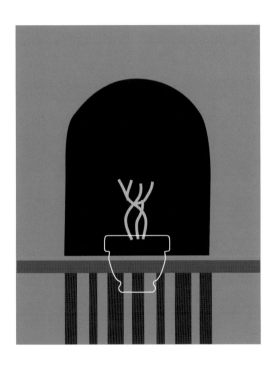

4. Appliqué the ivy leaves, then the topiary fruit and leaves in numerical order.

Embroider the Details

Note: Refer to "Embroidery Stitches" on pages 12–13 for stitch diagrams. Refer to the project photo and pattern for placement.

1. Using 2 strand of light green floss, chain-stitch the ivy vines and buttonhole-stitch around the edges of selected ivy leaves. Chain-stitch down the middle of 5 leaves on the topiary top.
2. Using 2 strands of dark green floss, chain-stitch down the middle of 3 leaves on the topiary top.
3. Using 2 strands of rust floss, satin-stitch the border design on the pot.
4. Using 2 strands of brown floss, buttonhole-stitch one edge of one trunk and satin-stitch 2 pear stems. Couch 4 strands of floss to the orange for the navel.
5. Using 2 strands of pink floss, sew running stitches on the rose grapes.
6. Using 2 strands of purple floss, buttonhole-stitch selected lavender and blue plums.

Frame the Design

Note: Refer to "Framing Your Design" on pages 11–12 for general instructions.

Have a professional framer frame the piece, padding it with the fleece.

Mixed Fruit Topiary Wall Hanging Pattern

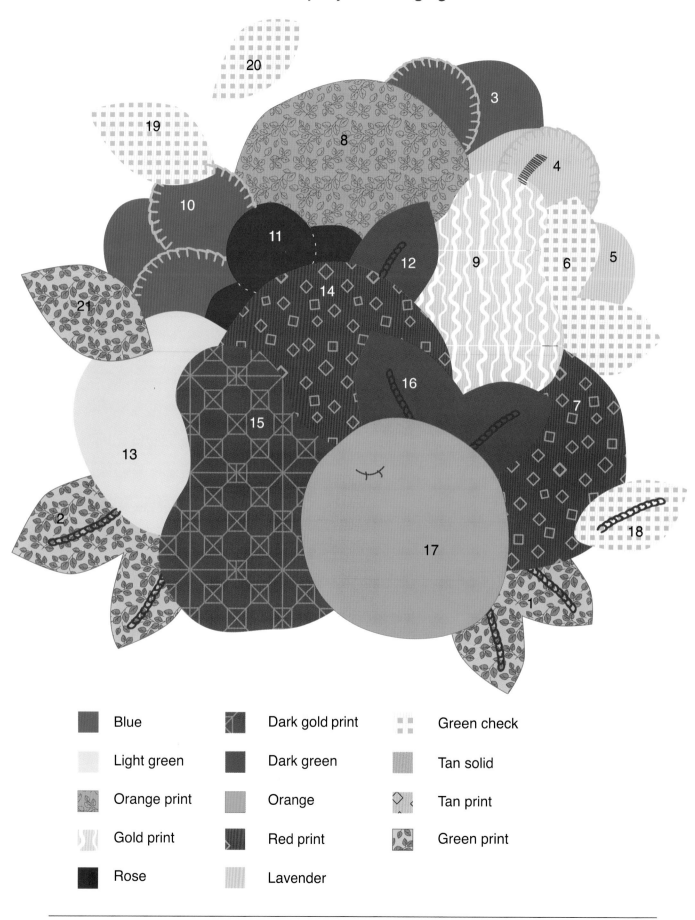

■ Blue	■ Dark gold print	▦ Green check
■ Light green	■ Dark green	■ Tan solid
▨ Orange print	■ Orange	◇ Tan print
▦ Gold print	■ Red print	▨ Green print
■ Rose	■ Lavender	

Mixed Fruit Topiary Wall Hanging Pattern

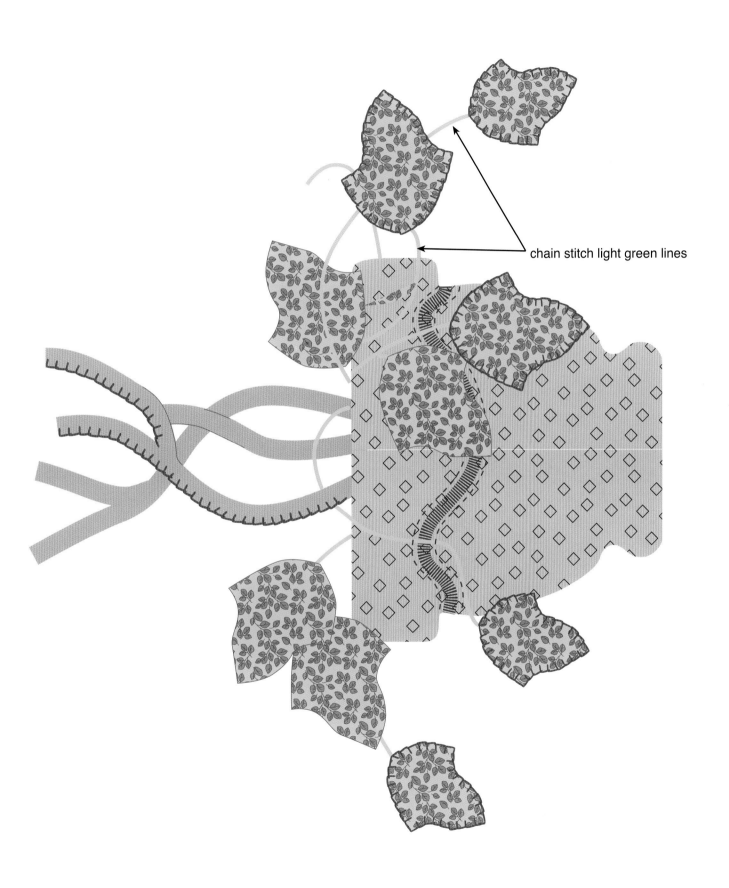

chain stitch light green lines

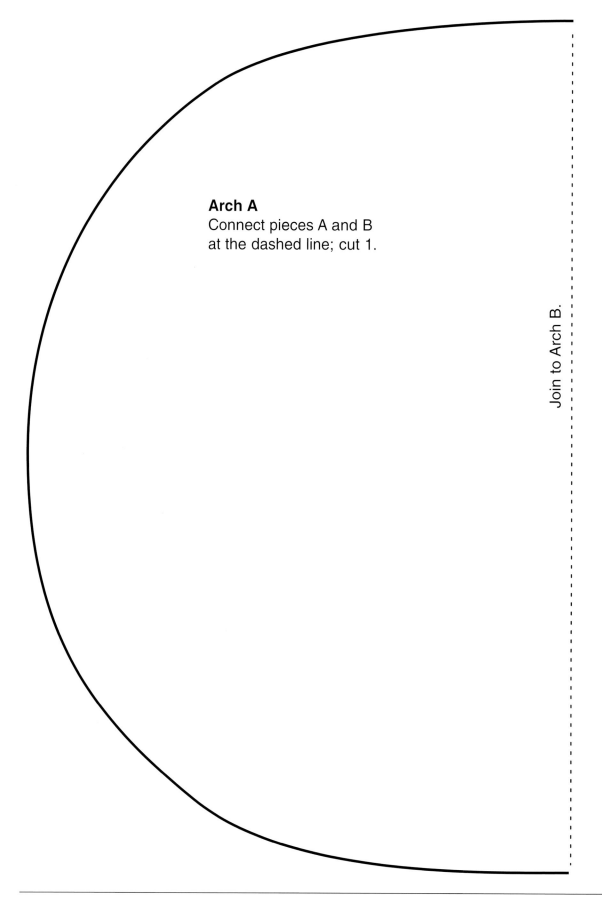

Arch A
Connect pieces A and B
at the dashed line; cut 1.

Join to Arch B.

Arch B

Join to Arch A.

Garden
Place Mat and Napkin

Finished Size:

Place mat: 18" x 12", Napkin: 18" x 18"

Materials for One Placemat

One 18" x 12" navy blue place mat
Scraps of cotton fabrics in these colors: tan,
  red, purple, light green, dark green, and
  green plaid
Navy blue embroidery floss
⅛ yard of paper-backed fusible web
Dark green permanent fabric marker
Tracing paper and pencil

Appliqué the Design

Note: Refer to "Fusible Appliqué" on pages 8–10 for general instructions. Refer to the project photo for placement.

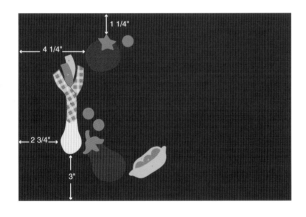

1. Trace the pattern pieces individually onto fusible web. Cut ½" from the drawn lines. Referring to the photo and color key, fuse the pattern pieces to the wrong sides of the corresponding fabrics and cut them out on the drawn lines.
2. Peel the paper backing off the red tomato and position it on the place mat, fusible side down. Fuse the tomato in place, following the manufacturer's directions. Fuse the dark green tomato top, then the green grape next to the tomato.

3. Fuse the leek, following the number sequence on the pattern. Fuse the 2 green grapes next to the leek.
4. Fuse the eggplant, then the green stem.
5. Fuse the pea pod and peas, following the number sequence on the pattern.

Add the Details

1. Using 1 strand of navy blue embroidery floss, make small tack stitches around the large fused pieces.
2. Using the green fabric marker, draw the shine mark on the eggplant.

Materials for One Napkin

One 18" x 18" navy blue napkin
Scraps of cotton fabrics in these colors: red
  and dark green
Navy blue embroidery floss
Scrap of paper-backed fusible web
Tracing paper and pencil

Appliqué the Design

Note: Refer to "Fusible Appliqué" on pages 8–10 for general instructions. Refer to the project photo for placement.

1. Trace the pattern pieces individually onto fusible web. Referring to the photo and color key, fuse the pattern pieces to the wrong side of the corresponding fabrics and cut them out on the drawn line.
2. Peel the paper backing off the red tomato and position it in a corner of the napkin, fusible side down. Fuse in place, following the manufacturer's directions. Fuse the dark green tomato top in place.
3. Using 1 strand of navy blue embroidery floss, make small tack stitches around the tomato's edge.

Garden Place Mat and Napkin Pattern

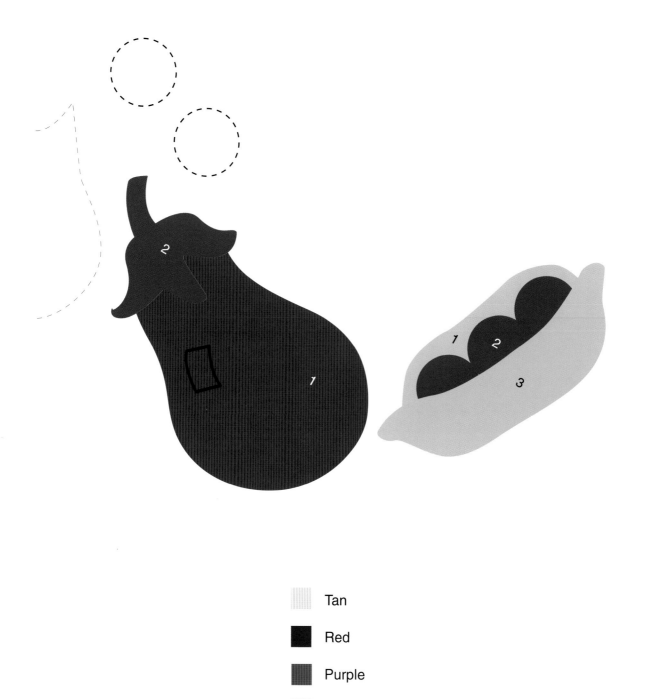

	Tan
	Red
	Purple
	Light green
	Dark green
	Green plaid

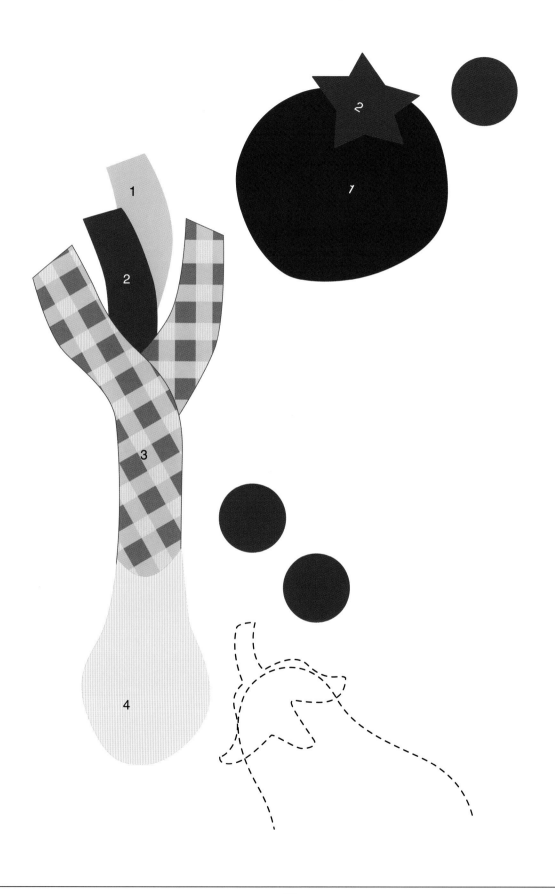

Teapot Wall Hanging

Finished Size: 10" x 14¼"

Materials

Scraps of cotton fabric in these colors: tan,
  light brown print, light blue print, blue
  print, yellow, turquoise, green check, pink,
  rose, light green, green print, lavender
  print, white, purple print, aqua, and purple
8¾" x 11½" blue/yellow print for center
  section of background
3¼" x 11½" blue/navy print for bottom
  section of background
Thread to match fabrics
Yellow embroidery floss
⅛ yard of paper-backed fusible web
Tracing paper and pencil
Air-soluble marking pen
Permanent fabric markers in these colors:
  purple, pink, and green

Prepare the Background

1. From each of the tan and light brown prints,
   cut 12 strips, each 5½" long, varying the
   widths between ⅞" and 1¼".
2. Stitch the strips together, alternating colors
   and using ¼"-wide seam allowances, to
   make a piece that is at least 5½" x 11½".
3. Trim the seam allowances slightly on the
   narrow strips. Press.
4. Stitch the tan/brown strip unit to an 11½"
   edge of the blue/yellow print background.

5. Stitch the blue/navy print to the bottom of
   the blue/yellow print. Press. The finished
   background should measure 11½" x 16".

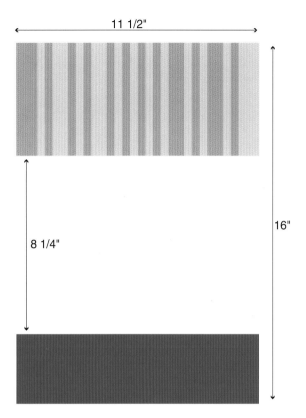

Appliqué the Design

Note: Refer to "Needle-Turn Appliqué" and "Fusible Appliqué" on pages 8–10 for general instructions. Refer to the project photos and pattern for placement.

1. Trace these pattern pieces onto fusible web: bird's feet, scallops for tea cups, teapot stems/leaves, scallops for teapot, and "shine" spot for teapot. Cut ½" from the drawn lines and fuse to the wrong side of the corresponding fabric scraps; set aside.

2. Trace the remaining pattern pieces onto tracing paper, adding ¼" seam allowances. Referring to the photo and color key, pin the patterns to the corresponding fabrics and cut on the outer marked lines.

3. Appliqué the 2 saucers, then the inner and outer cups. Above the left cup, appliqué the bird's body and its wing. In the right cup, appliqué the leaves, then the flower, and fuse the stem.

4. Referring to the illustration below, mark the teapot placement on the background. Cut out the teapot stems/leaves. Peel off the paper backing and fuse in place.

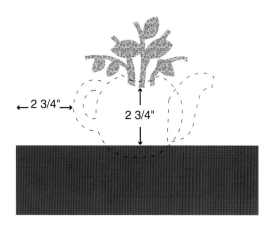

5. Appliqué the turquoise teapot spout, then the lavender print spout. Appliqué the teapot, then the flowers, beginning with the purple-and-turquoise flower in the center.

6. Cut out and fuse the bird's feet, the scallops on the teacups, and the scallops and shine on the teapot.

Add the Details

Note: Refer to "Embroidery Stitches" on pages 12–13 for stitch diagrams. Refer to the project photo and the patterns for placement.

1. Using 2 strands of yellow embroidery floss, make a French knot for the bird's eye and satin-stitch its beak. Sew running stitches to make stamens in the turquoise section of the center flower.

2. With the purple fabric marker, make small circles in the centers of the pink, yellow, and turquoise flowers. With the green fabric marker, make 2 small circles at the ends of the running stitches in the center flower. With the pink fabric marker, make single circles in the centers of the rose flowers.

3. Using the air-soluble marking pen, mark a 1" grid on the yellow/blue background. At the intersections, make plus marks with the pink fabric marker; refer to the photo for placement.

Teapot Wall Hanging Pattern

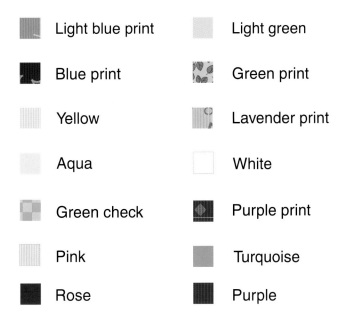

Light blue print	Light green
Blue print	Green print
Yellow	Lavender print
Aqua	White
Green check	Purple print
Pink	Turquoise
Rose	Purple

Tea Wall Plaques

Finished Size: 6" x 9⅛"

Materials

Each Wall Plaque
9" x 9" piece of medium blue felt for background
5½" x 8½" piece of coordinating fabric for back
Thread to match fabrics
Tracing paper and pencil
6" x 12" piece of fusible web
6" x 9" piece of foam-core board
Air-soluble or water-soluble marking pen
Craft glue (optional)

Echinacea Wall Plaque
9" x 5" piece of blue/tan check for lower border
Scraps of fabric in these colors: dark blue print, green check, bright pink check, and dark brown print
Embroidery floss in these colors: light green, tan, and blue
12" piece of purple paper twist

Ginseng Wall Plaque
9" x 5" piece of navy blue print for lower border
Scraps of fabric in these colors: light blue, green check, green print, and red
Embroidery floss in these colors: light green and teal
12" piece of green paper twist

Mint Wall Plaque
9" x 5" piece of blue print for lower border
Scraps of fabric in these colors: orange print, mint green, green, and lavender
Embroidery floss in these colors: light green, lavender, and dark green
12" length of purple paper twist

Chamomile Wall Plaque
9" x 5" piece of black/tan check fabric for lower border
Scraps of fabric in these colors: gold print, light green print, dark green print, white, and yellow print
Embroidery floss in these colors: light green, dark brown, dark green, and gold
12" length of green paper twist

Appliqué the Design

Note: Refer to "Needle-Turn Appliqué" and "Fusible Appliqué" on pages 8–10. Refer to the project photos and pattern for appliqué placement.

1. For each wall plaque, trace the cup (pages 66–69) onto tracing paper, adding ¼" seam allowances. Referring to the photo and color key, pin the cup to the corresponding fabric and cut on the outer marked line.
2. Make a pattern overlay (pages 8–9). Use the overlay to trace the remaining pattern pieces onto fusible web. Cut ½" from the drawn lines. Fuse the pieces to the wrong sides of the corresponding fabric scraps.
3. Pin the overlay to the felt and leave it in place throughout the appliqué process.

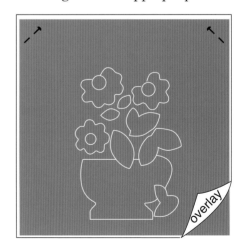

4. Appliqué the cup to the felt, ¾" from the bottom edge, using traditional appliqué.
5. Fuse the appliqué pieces for each wall plaque as follows:

Echinacea

1. Cut out the leaves. Peel off the paper backing and place the leaves on the felt, fusible side down, using the pattern overlay as a guide for placement. Fuse the leaves in place.

2. Cut out and fuse the flowers, then the flower centers. Discard the pattern overlay.

Ginseng

1. Cut out the 2 large green check leaves and the 2 green print leaves. Peel off the paper backing and place the leaves on the felt, fusible side down, using the overlay as a guide for placement. Fuse the leaves in place.

2. Cut out and fuse the remaining leaves and the red berries. Discard the overlay.

Mint

1. Cut out the 3 lower green leaves. Peel off the paper backing and place on the felt, fusible side down, using the overlay as a guide for placement. Fuse the pieces. Cut out and fuse the leaves that overlap the cup.

2. Cut out and fuse the remaining green and mint green leaves and the lavender flowers. Discard the overlay.

Chamomile

1. Cut out the light green print leaves. Peel off the paper backing and place the leaves on the felt, fusible side down, using the pattern overlay as a guide for placement. Fuse the leaves in place.

2. Cut out and fuse the dark green print leaf, then the white flowers and yellow flower centers. Discard the overlay.

Embroider the Details

Note: Refer to "Embroidery Stitches" on pages 12–13 for stitch diagrams. Refer to the project photo and pattern for placement.

Mark the embroidery lines for your wall plaque with an air-soluble or water-soluble pen as follows:

Echinacea

Using 2 strands of light green floss, chain-stitch the stems and make French knots in the flower centers. Using 2 strands of tan floss, back-stitch the word "Echinacea." Using 2 strands of blue floss, make a running stitch to mark the inner cup handle

Ginseng

Using 2 strands of light green floss, chain-stitch the stems. Make 1 French knot in 5 berry centers. Using 2 strands of teal floss, backstitch the word "Ginseng."

Mint

Using 2 strands of light green floss, chain-stitch the flower stems. Using 2 strands of lavender floss, satin-stitch the circles on the flowers. Using 2 strands of dark green floss, backstitch the word "Mint."

Chamomile

Using 2 strands of light green floss, chain-stitch the flower stems. Using 2 strands of dark brown floss, make long stitches that radiate from the flower centers, then make 1 French knot in each flower center. Using 2 strands of dark green floss, backstitch the word "Chamomile." Using 2 strands of gold floss, make a running stitch to mark the inner cup handle.

Make the Wall Plaque

1. Sew the lower border fabric to the bottom of the appliqué piece, matching the 9" sides and using a ¼" seam allowance.
2. Lay the assembled piece face down and center the foam-core board over it. Pull the edges snugly to the back and stitch or glue in place.
3. Cut fusible web and apply to the wrong side of the backing fabric. Peel off the paper backing and place the fabric on the wall plaque, fusible side down. Fuse in place.
4. Bend the paper twist into an arch and whip-stitch the ends to the sides of the wall plaque at the top; see photos on pages 60–61.

Echinacea Wall Plaque Pattern

Dark brown print

Green check

Bright pink print

Dark blue print

Ginseng Wall Plaque Pattern

Light blue

Green check

Green print

Red

Mint Wall Plaque Pattern

Orange print

Mint green

Green

Lavender

Chamomile Wall Plaque Pattern

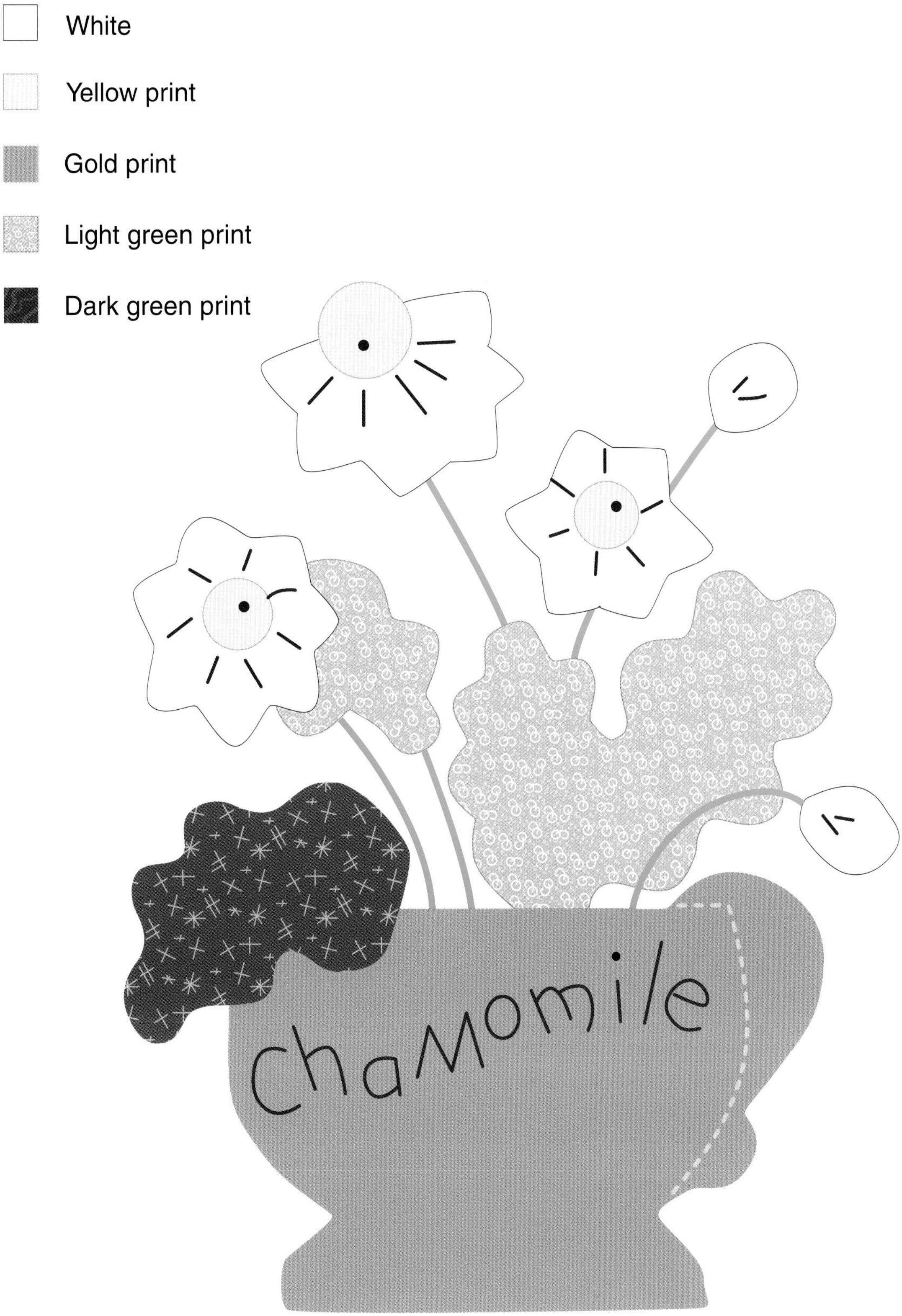

☐ White

▦ Yellow print

▦ Gold print

▦ Light green print

▦ Dark green print

Cat in the Garden Pillow

Finished Size: 19" x 17"

Materials

⅝ yard of 44"-wide brown check fabric
17" x 19" piece of blue plaid fabric
14" x 16" piece of cream felt
9" x 12" piece of teal felt
12" x 14" piece of fusible web
Scraps of cotton fabric in these colors: light
   rust, dark brown print, navy/white print,
   brown/tan check, blue, gold print, dark
   brown solid, white, orange, dark green,
   purple, bright pink check, medium brown,
   green print, and red print
Thread to match fabrics
Navy blue embroidery floss
Polyester fiberfill
3 assorted ½"- to ⅝"-diameter buttons
Tracing paper and pencil
Air-soluble or water-soluble marking pen

Appliqué the Design

*Note: refer to "Needle-Turn Appliqué" and "Fusible
Appliqué" on pages 8–10 for general instructions. Refer to
the project photo and pattern for appliqué placement.*

1. Trace the rounded rectangles (pages 76–79)
   onto tracing paper, adding ¼" seam allowances. Referring to the photo and color key,
   pin the patterns to the gold print fabric and
   cut on the outer marked lines.

2. Trace the remaining pattern pieces individually onto fusible web, including the back-
   grounds for the hearts and cherries. Cut ½"
   from the drawn lines and fuse the pieces to
   the wrong sides of the corresponding fabric
   scraps, using the photo and patterns as
   guides. Cut out the pieces on the marked lines.

3. Remove the paper backing from the light
   rust house piece and place it on the teal felt,
   fusible side down. Fuse the house in place.
   Fuse the roof piece, then the chimney pieces
   and the door.

4. To fuse the basket, position the brown/tan
   check and the blue center pieces on the teal
   felt. Tuck the right-hand handle underneath
   the blue fabric. Fuse both pieces at once.

5. Fuse the beehive to the teal felt, then fuse
   the door.

6. Fuse the butterfly wings to the teal felt, then
   fuse the body.

7. Fuse the flower's leaves to the teal felt, then
   fuse the flower and the flower center.

8. Fuse the cat to the teal felt, then the stripes.

9. Fuse the cotton hearts to the felt heart piece,
   then fuse the cotton cherries and leaves to
   the cherry felt piece.

10. After the fusing is complete, trim the felt
    background of each piece to within ⅛" of
    the fused pieces, excpet fo the heart and
    cherries. Set design pieces aside.

11. Appliqué the tan print pieces to the cream
    felt background, using needle-turn appliqué.

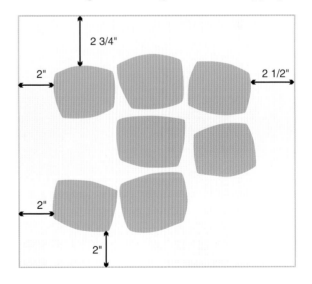

12. Place the design pieces on the background
    and appliqué in place, referring to the dia-
    gram on page 73.

Add the Details

Note: Refer to "Embroidery Stitches" on pages 12–13 for stitch diagrams. Refer to the project photo and pattern for placement.

1. Using 2 strands of navy blue floss, sew running stitches on the large heart, the beehive, and the cat's tail and legs. Backstitch the cat's face, satin-stitch the cat's nose, and make French knots for the eyes.
2. Sew the buttons near the center of the design as shown in the photo.

Assemble the Pillow

1. From the brown check fabric, cut 2 pieces, each 18" x 20", for the flange and back of the pillow. Stitch the two pieces with right sides together, leaving an opening in one edge. Trim the corners and turn. Stitch around the pillow 2" from the edge, leaving an opening in the same side as before.

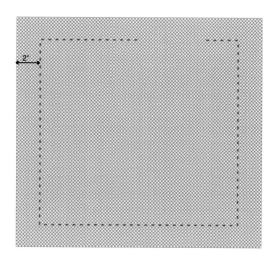

2. Stuff the pillow firmly with fiberfill. Stitch both of the openings closed.
3. Center the blue plaid fabric and the pillow front over the front of the brown check pillow and pin. Sew the two fabric pieces to the pillow, using a zipper foot and stitching over the inside seam. Trim the cream felt right next to the stitching line.

4. Trace the pointed border pattern on page 79 onto tracing paper and cut it out. Pin it over the blue plaid border at the corner of the pillow; cut points around the edge of the blue plaid piece. Note that the points are irregular. Repeat at the remaining corners, flipping the pattern over as necessary.

Light rust

Dark brown print

Navy blue print

Brown/Tan check

Blue

Gold print

Dark brown

White

Orange

Dark green

Purple

Bright pink print

Brown

Green print

Red print

Teal felt

Placement Reference Diagram
(not shown actual size)

Cat in the Garden Pillow Pattern

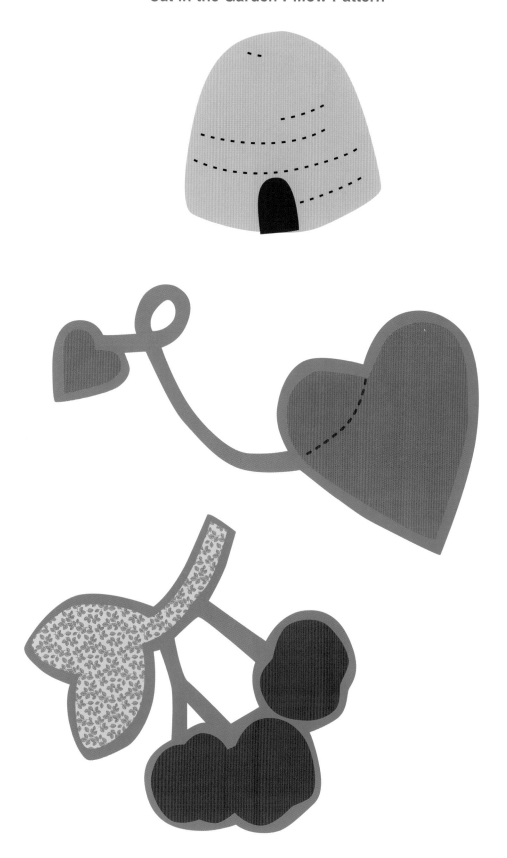

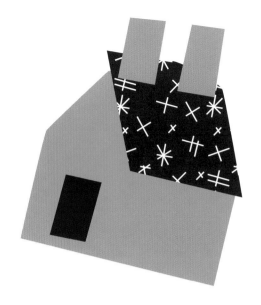

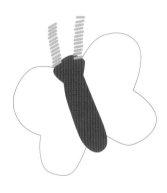

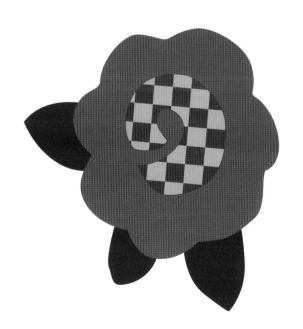

Cat in the Garden Pillow Pattern

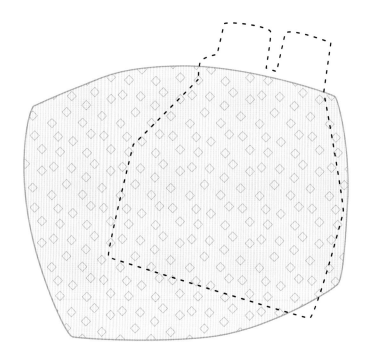

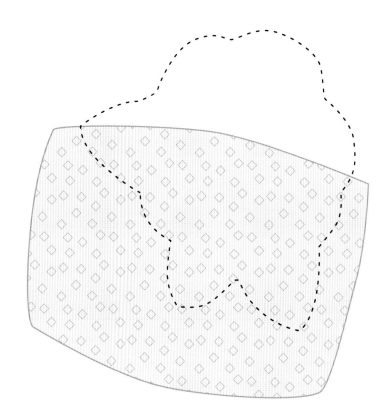

Cat in the Garden Pillow Pattern

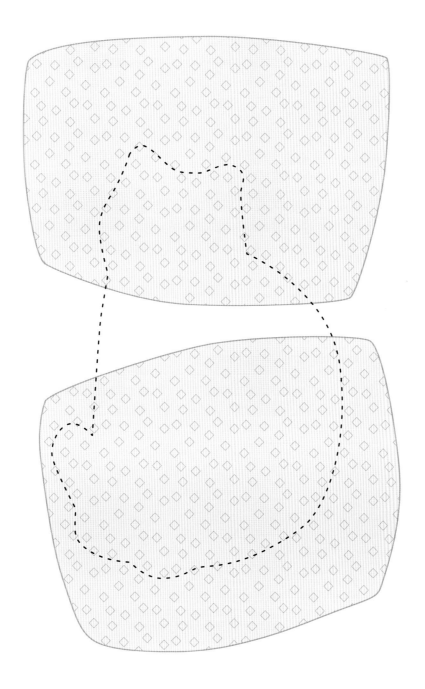

Cat in the Garden Pillow Pattern

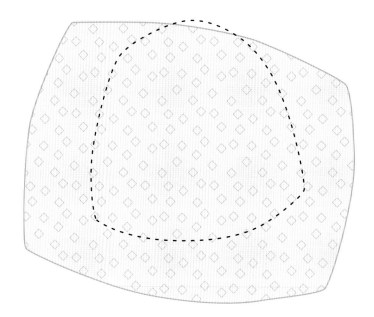

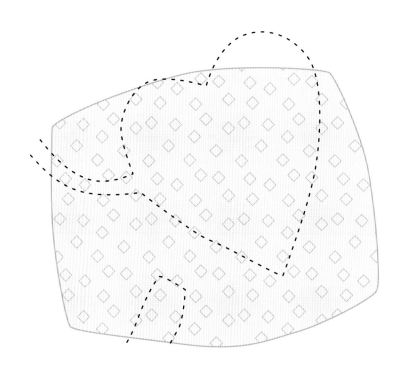

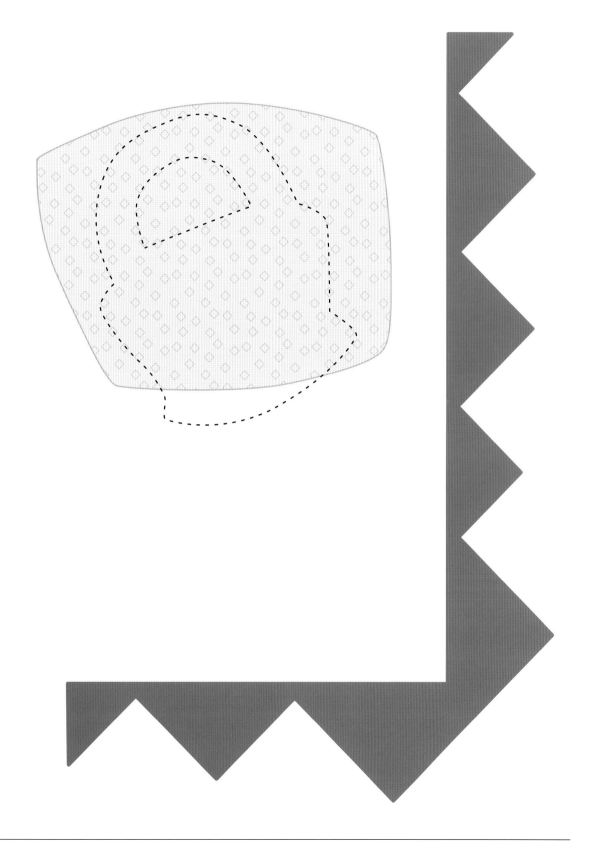

Wreath Pillows

Cream Wreath Pillow

Orange Wreath Pillow

Finished Size: 7¾" x 7¾"

Materials

Thread to match fabrics
Gold embroidery floss
10" x 10" piece of paper-backed fusible web
Tracing paper and pencil
Air-soluble or water-soluble pen
Polyester fiberfill
For cream pillow:
    8" x 16" piece of tan felt for pillow front
      and back
    7" x 7" piece of cream cotton fabric
    Scraps of fabric in these colors: Light
      green, purple, red/purple print, rose,
      gold and turquoise
For orange pillow:
    8" x 16" piece of orange felt for pillow
      front and back
    7" x 7" piece of blue chambray cotton
      fabric
    Scraps of fabric in these colors: teal, red,
      orange, dark red print, turquoise,
      and gold

Appliqué the Design

Note: Refer to "Needle-Turn Appliqué" on page 8 for general instructions. Refer to the project photo, pattern, and diagrams for appliqué placement.

The following instructions are for the cream pillow. To make the orange wreath pillow, use the patterns on page 87 and follow the instructions below, substituting the fabrics shown on the orange wreath pillow placement diagram and color key.

1. Trace the pattern pieces (page 85) onto tracing paper, adding ¼" seam allowances. Referring to the photo and color key, pin the patterns to the corresponding fabrics and cut on the outer marked lines.

2. Fold the cream square into quarters and mark the center. Use an air- or water-soluble marking pen to mark a 5"-wide circle in the middle of the square.

3. Using the circle for placement, pin 1 small rose piece and the 5 light green leaf pieces onto the fabric. The leaves are numbered for easy placement. Appliqué the pieces.

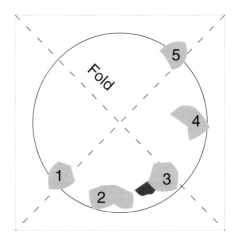

4. Appliqué 2 small purple pieces, then 1 large rose flower. Appliqué the 2 red/purple print pieces on the left side of the floral wreath.

5. Appliqué the 2 large purple flowers, then the red/purple print flower, the large rose flower, and the remaining leaf piece.

6. Appliqué the 3 small gold circles and the 2 turquoise circles.

Embroider the Details

Note: Refer to "Embroidery Stitches" on pages 12–13 for stitch diagrams. Refer to the project photo and diagram for placement.

1. Mark the embroidery placement lines with an air-soluble or water-soluble pen.
2. Using 2 strands of gold floss, chain-stitch the curves in the flowers and the center lines on the leaves.

Finish the Pillow

1. From the tan felt, cut two 8" x 8" pieces.
2. Trim the appliqué piece to 6" x 6" with the design centered. Center the design on one piece of tan felt. Turn under the raw edges and appliqué to the felt square.
3. Stitch the pillow front and the pillow back together, using a ¼" seam allowance and leaving an opening in one edge. Stuff with fiberfill. Slipstitch the opening closed.

Cream Wreath Pillow Placement Diagram

▨	Light green
▨	Turquoise
▨	Rose
▨	Purple
▨	Red/Purple print
▨	Gold

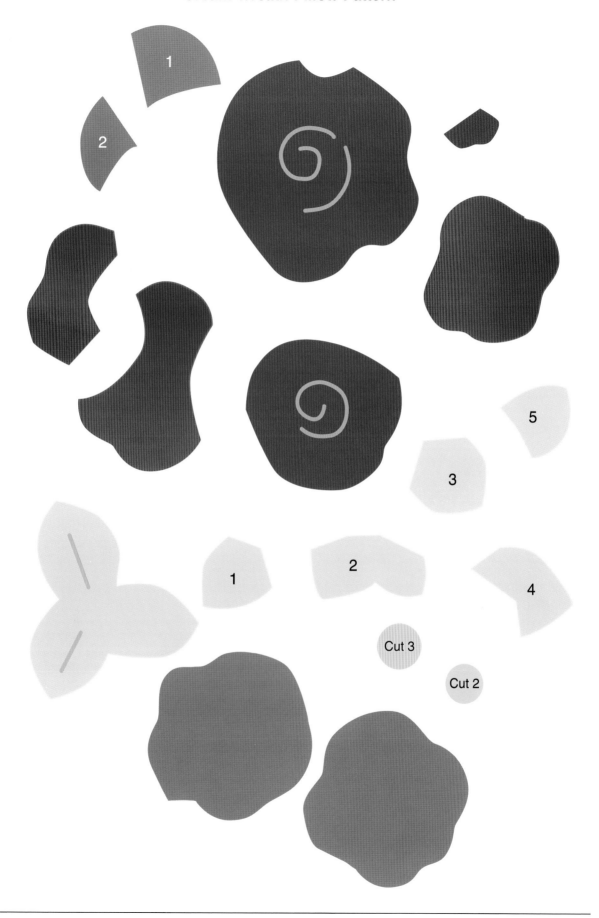

Orange Wreath Pillow Placement Diagram

Teal

Red

Orange

Dark red print

Turquoise

Gold

Orange Wreath Pillow Pattern

Cut 3

Cut 2

5

1

4

2

1

3

2

Sunshine Wall Hanging

Finished Size: 15" x 17½"

Materials

¼ yard of 44"-wide blue plaid for border
⅛ yard of 44"-wide black/rust print for
  border
8" x 12" piece light brown fabric for center
  section
Scraps of cotton fabric in these colors: gold
  print, yellow, blue print, lavender, green
  print, dark green, light green, green plaid,
  purple, tan solid, red, bright yellow, orange
  check, orange print, tan print, blue-green,
  navy/white print, burgundy, light green
  print, blue/navy print, and red check
Thread to match fabrics
Embroidery floss in these colors: tan, bright
  green, pale lavender, and charcoal
16" x 18" piece of tan felt for backing
¼ yard of paper-backed fusible web
¼"-diameter dowel, 13½" long
Tracing paper and pencil
Air-soluble marking pen
Colored pencils
Dark green permanent fabric marker
Pinking shears

Prepare the Background

1. From the navy/white print, cut 2 pieces,
   each 1¼" x 2½". From the burgundy fabric,
   cut 1 piece, 1¼" x 2½". Sew the long edges
   of the pieces together, with the burgundy
   strip in the center and using ¼" seam
   allowances. Cut in half.

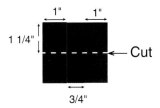

2. From the blue-green fabric, cut 2 pieces,
   each 2¾" x 7¼". Sew a navy/burgundy
   unit to one short end of each blue-green
   fabric piece.

Make 2.

3. From the blue plaid fabric, cut 2 strips, each
   ⅞" x 8"; set aside remaining plaid fabric.
   Sew the blue plaid strip to the inside edges
   of the blue-green pieces.

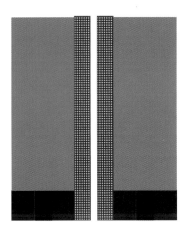

4. From the light brown fabric, cut 1 piece, 6¾" x 11⅝", for the center section. Sew the pieced side sections to the light brown center section, aligning the bottom edges. From the tan print, cut 2 top corner pieces, using the pattern on page 92. Place the top corner pieces over the pieced sections, aligning outside edges, and pin. Turn under the curved edges of the tan print pieces and slipstitch in place. The outside edges of the block will measure 12" wide and 11⅝" long.

5. To make the pieced bottom strip, cut 1 of each of these pieces: from light green print, 2¾" x 2⅞", from tan print, 2⅞" x 5", from blue/navy print, 2⅞" x 3", and from red check, 2¾" x 2⅞". Sew the 2⅞" edges together in the order shown in the photo. Sew the pieced strip to the bottom edge of the pieced upper section, aligning seams.

6. From the blue plaid fabric, cut 2 pieces, each 1¾" x 15", and 1 piece, 1¾" x 12". Sew the 1¾" x 12" piece to the top edge of the pieced section. Then sew the 2 remaining strips to the sides, aligning the bottom edges. The outside edges may not match.

7. From the black/rust print, cut 1 piece, 2¾" x 15". Sew it to the bottom edge of the pieced section. The outside edges may not match but will be trimmed later.

Appliqué the Design

Note: Refer to "Fusible Appliqué" on pages 8–10 for general instructions. Refer to the project photo and pattern for appliqué placement.

1. Trace the pattern pieces on pages 93–97 onto the fusible web. Cut ½" from the sun pieces. Fuse pieces to the wrong sides of the sun fabrics. Cut on the marked lines. Peel off the paper backing and place the sun's rays on the background; see photo for placement. Fuse the rays in place, then fuse the sun's face and the blue print band in the same manner.
2. Cut out and fuse the purple eggplant, then the dark green top. Cut out and fuse the leek, following the number sequence on the pattern.
3. Cut out and fuse the upper tomato. Cut out and fuse the cauliflower, following the number sequence on the pattern.
4. Cut out and fuse the orange check carrot, then the orange print carrot.
5. Cut out and fuse the "sunshine" lettering.
6. Cut out and fuse the cabbage, following the number sequence on the pattern. Cut out and fuse the lower tomato, then its top. Cut out and fuse the pea pod, following the number sequence on the pattern. Cut out and fuse the pepper, then the top. Fuse the remaining peas; see photo for placement.

Add the Details

Note: Refer to "Embroidery Stitches" on pages 12–13 for stitch diagrams. Refer to the project photo and pattern for placement.

1. Transfer the embroidery lines for the sun's face and the "good day" lettering.
2. Using 2 strands of charcoal floss, backstitch the nose, eyes, and mouth on the sun. Tack-stitch the yellow and blue edges of the sun, using tan embroidery floss around the sun's rays and charcoal floss around the blue print band. Use colored pencils to add colors to the eyelids, eyes, cheeks, and mouth. Using 2 strands of tan floss, tack-stitch the outside edges of the sun's rays.
3. Using 2 strands of bright green embroidery floss, stem-stitch the lettering. Using 2 strands of pale lavender floss, tack-stitch the appliquéd letters.
4. Using 2 strands of charcoal floss, tack-stitch the edges of all the vegetables.
5. Use the permanent marker to add the lines on the eggplant, leek, cabbage, pepper, cauliflower, and carrots.

Finish the Wall Hanging

1. Mark the blue plaid pieces 1¼" from the seams. Mark the black/rust piece 2⅛" from the seam. Trim the design piece on the marked lines, using pinking shears. Center the design piece over the tan felt. Baste.
2. Quilt around the sun, the sun's rays, and the appliquéd lettering. Quilt near the seams joining the tan print corner pieces. Quilt along the inner edges of the light brown center section and around the inner edges of the blue-green pieced blocks on the sides. Quilt along the inner edges of the borders, quilting around any vegetables extending into the borders as you come to them. Quilt 2 parallel rows of stitching in the border; see the photo.
3. To make a hanging sleeve, cut a 1½" x 14" strip of blue plaid. Fold the short raw edges under twice and hem. Fold the strip in half lengthwise, right sides together. Stitch a ¼" seam allowance on the long edge. Turn right side out. Slipstitch the sleeve to the top edge of the wall hanging back. Insert the dowel. Tack the bottom edge of the sleeve to the wall hanging back.

Sunshine Wall Hanging Pattern

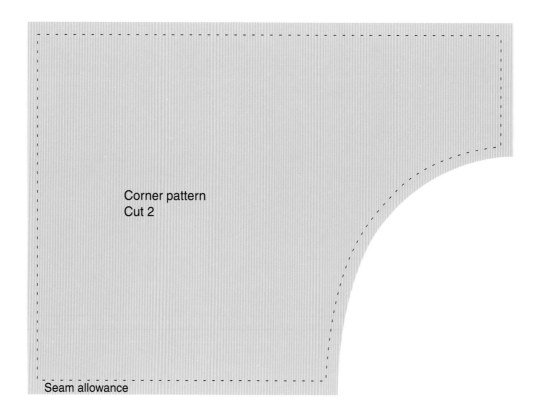

Corner pattern
Cut 2

Seam allowance

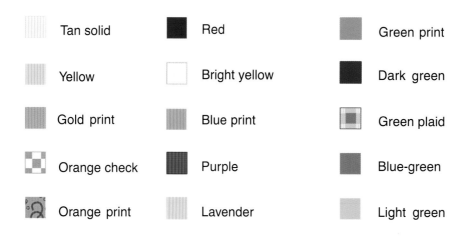

Tan solid	Red	Green print
Yellow	Bright yellow	Dark green
Gold print	Blue print	Green plaid
Orange check	Purple	Blue-green
Orange print	Lavender	Light green

GooD-
day
Sunshine

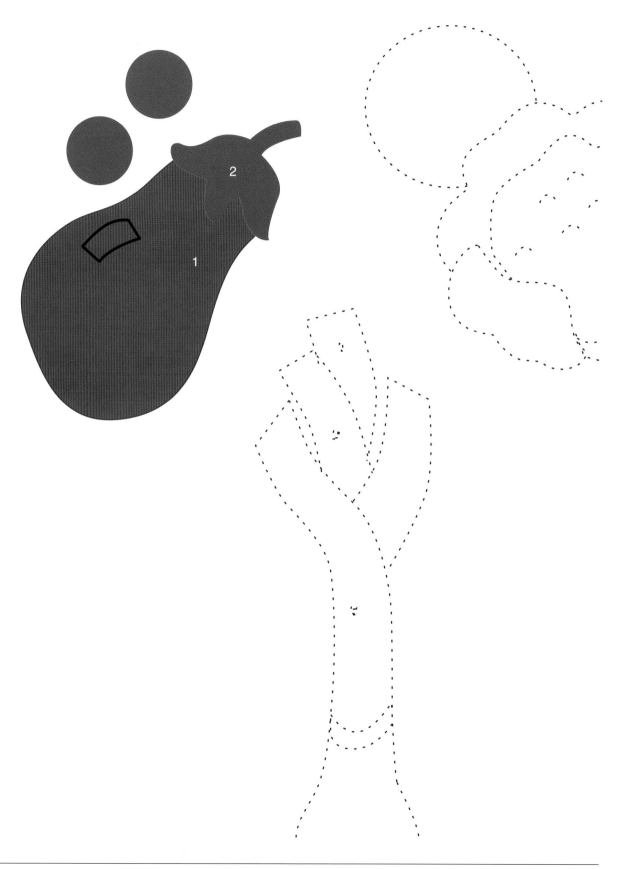

Autumn Leaves Wall Hanging

Finished Size: 14" x 19"

Materials

⅝ yard of 44"-wide brown print for border and backing

½ yard of 44"-wide rust for background

Scraps of cotton fabric in these colors: light green print, dark green print, rust print, brown stripe, burgundy print, gold print, gold solid, brown/black print, and tan

Thread to match fabrics

Embroidery floss in these colors: cream, tan, bright green, charcoal, and white

14" x 19" piece of polyester fleece

¼ yard of paper-backed fusible web

5 buttons in assorted sizes and colors

¼"-diameter dowel, 13" long

Tracing paper and pencil

Air-soluble or water-soluble marking pen

Appliqué the Design

Note: Refer to "Fusible Appliqué" on pages 8–10 for general instructions. Refer to the project photo and pattern for appliqué placement.

1. Cut a 14" x 19" piece of rust fabric for the background.

2. Using the patterns on pages 102–105, make a pattern overlay for the design, following the instructions in "Fusible Appliqué" on pages 8–9. You may need to tape together pieces of tracing paper to make a sheet large enough.

3. Use the pattern overlay to trace the pattern pieces for all the leaves and the small rust print block onto the fusible web. Cut ½" from the drawn lines. Referring to the photo and the color key, fuse the pattern pieces to the wrong sides of the corresponding fabrics. Pin the overlay to the background and leave it in place throughout the appliqué process.

4. Trace the remaining block background patterns onto tracing paper, drawing the full block when one is overlapped by another. Referring to the photo and color key, pin the patterns to the corresponding fabrics and cut on the marked lines. (The edges of these pieces will not be turned under.)

5. Cut the rust print block on the drawn lines. Peel off the paper backing and place the web on the background, fusible side down, using the pattern overlay as a guide. Fuse to the background.

6. Using the pattern overlay as a guide, cut out and fuse the gold print and rust leaves to the lower light green print block. Also cut out and fuse the gold solid leaf to the lower brown stripe block. Layer the green print and the lower brown stripe blocks over the burgundy print blocks. Baste to the background.

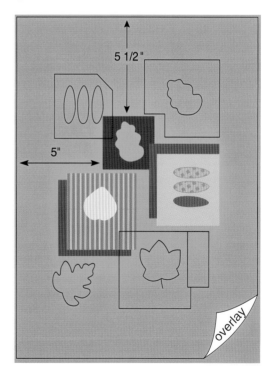

7. Referring to the photo and color key, cut out and fuse the remaining leaves—except the brown/black print leaf—to the blocks. Place the blocks on the background and baste in place. Cut out and fuse the brown/black print leaf to the background. Remove the overlay.

Embroider the Details

Note: Refer to "Embroidery Stitches" on pages 12–13 for stitch diagrams. Refer to the project photo and pattern for placement.

1. Using 2 strands of cream embroidery floss, sew running stitches ⅛" inside and parallel to the edges of the upper light green print block, in the center of the rust print and the brown stripe leaves, and in a wave pattern on the right-hand burgundy print block. Stem-stitch the stems on the rust print and the brown stripe leaves. Backstitch the stems of the gold and rust leaves. Cross-stitch 3 large stitches on the left edge of the left-hand burgundy block.

2. Using 2 strands of charcoal floss, sew running stitches ⅛" inside and parallel to the edges of the large rust print block. Sew running stitches on the top, right, and bottom edges of the upper brown stripe block; tack-stitch the left-hand edge. Sew running stitches on 3 sides of the light green print block.

3. Using 2 strands of bright green floss, tack-stitch the edges of the lower brown stripe block. Sew running stitches in the center of the leaf and ⅛" inside and parallel to the edges of the tan block. Stem-stitch the stem on the gold leaf.

4. Using 2 strands of white floss, sew running stitches on the right edge of the lower light green print block.

Finish the Wall Hanging

1. From the backing fabric, cut 1 piece, 18" x 23", and 1 piece, 14" x 19". On the larger piece, mark 3¾" from all edges. Cut on the line to make the frame. Center the frame, right side up, over the design piece. Topstitch the frame to the design piece, using dark thread and stitching ⅛" from and parallel to the cut edge.

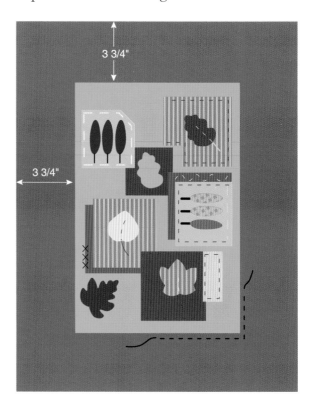

2. Place the smaller piece wrong side up on a flat surface. Layer the polyester fleece over it, then center the design piece on top, right side up; baste. Fold the frame to the back, turning under the raw edges. Slipstitch the edges of the frame piece to the back of the wall hanging.

3. Sew the buttons onto the wall hanging, using cream embroidery floss; see the photo for placement.

4. To make a hanging sleeve, cut a 1½" x 13" strip of brown print. Fold the short raw edges under twice and hem. Fold the strip in half lengthwise, right sides together. Stitch with a ¼" seam allowance on the long edge. Turn right side out. Slipstitch the sleeve to the top edge of the wall hanging back. Insert the dowel. Tack the bottom edge of the sleeve to the wall hanging back.

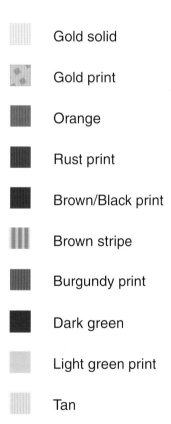

Gold solid

Gold print

Orange

Rust print

Brown/Black print

Brown stripe

Burgundy print

Dark green

Light green print

Tan

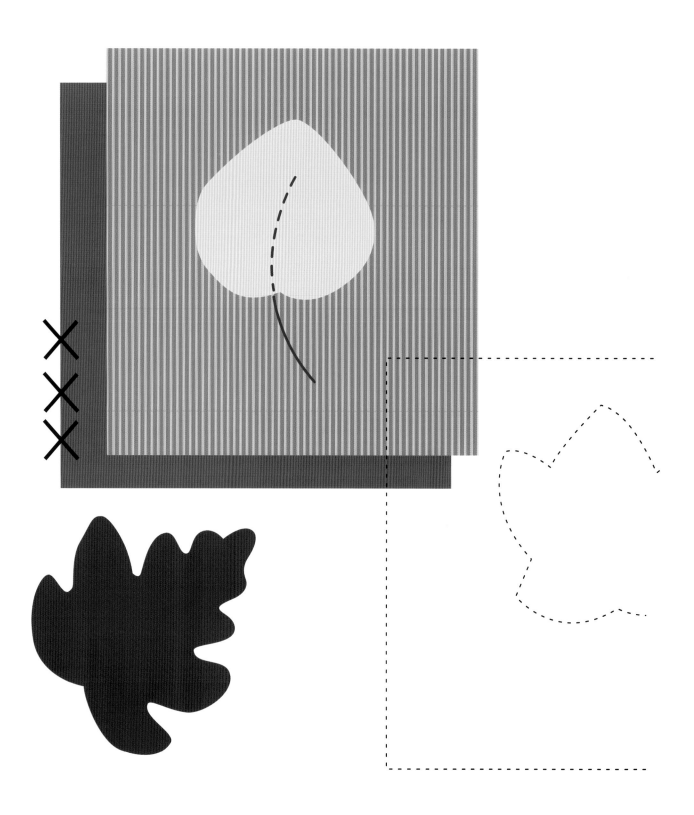

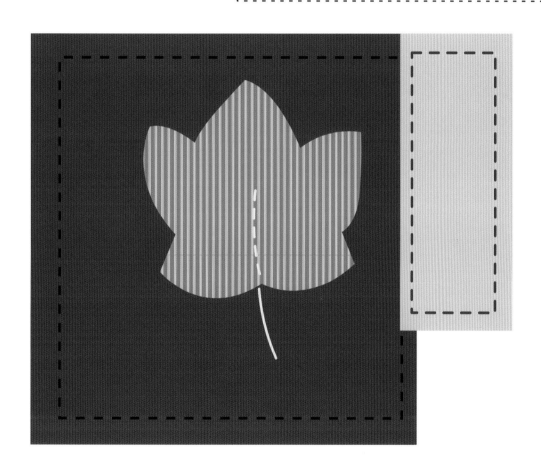

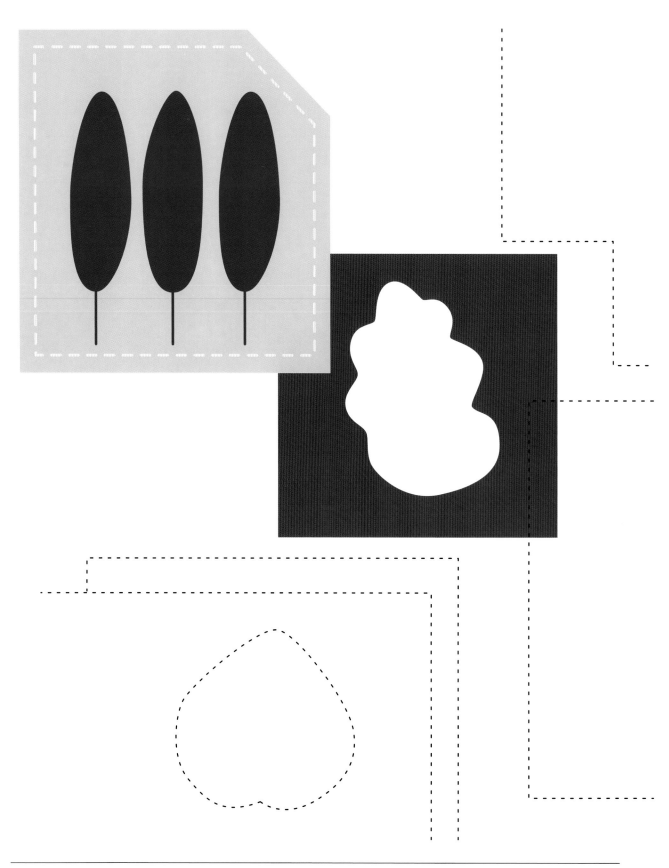

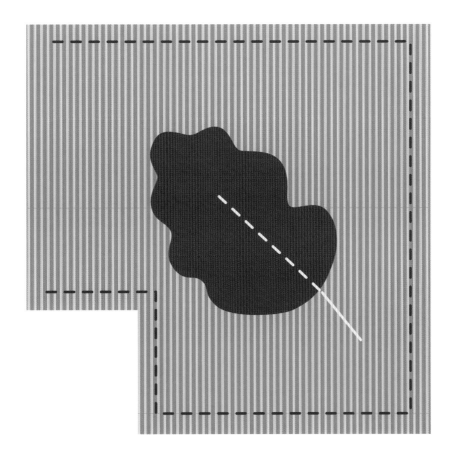

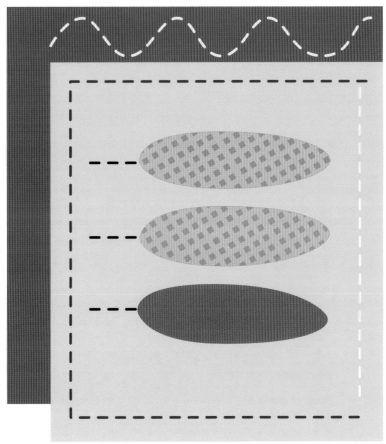

I Love My Garden
Wall Hanging

Finished Size: 13½" x 22"

Materials

18" x 28" piece of light blue check for background

Scraps of cotton fabric in these colors: navy blue plaid, blue print, turquoise, orange, yellow, green print, light green, dark green print, aqua, lavender, rose, brown, black print, yellow print, tan, light blue print, pink floral print, pink solid, small pink print, and bright pink print

Thread to match fabrics

Embroidery floss in these colors: turquoise, brown, bright pink, aqua, orange, navy blue, light blue, white, and very light blue

¼ yard of paper-backed fusible web

17" x 25" piece of polyester fleece

Buttons: 1 gray ¼"-diameter, 1 blue ½"-diameter, 3 brown ½"-diameter, 3 pink ⅝"-diameter, 1 cream ⅜" diameter

Bright pink acrylic paint

Small brush

Masking tape

Tracing paper

Pencil

Air-soluble or water-soluble marking pen

Appliqué the Design

Note: refer to "Needle-Turn Appliqué" and "Fusible Appliqué" on pages 8–10 for general instructions. Refer to the project photo and pattern for appliqué placement.

1. Trace the yellow arch and the bright pink print border of the dress (pages 110–111) onto tracing paper. For the yellow arch, do not add any seam allowances. For the pink border, add a ¼" seam allowance to the edge that tucks under the dress only. Pin the patterns to the corresponding fabrics and cut on the marked lines. (The edges of these pieces will not be turned under.)

2. Trace the remaining pattern pieces individually onto tracing paper, adding ¼" seam allowances. Referring to the photo and color key, pin the patterns to the corresponding fabrics and cut on the outer marked lines.

3. Use the paper patterns to plan the placement for the figure, tracing a few placement lines onto the fabric with the marking pen. Appliqué the shoes, then the pink floral print border of the dress. Baste the bright pink print border to the background. Follow the numbering sequence to complete the figure.

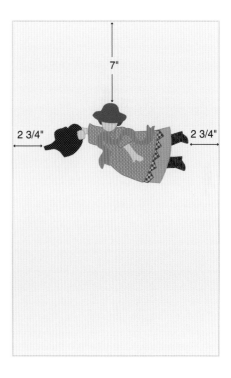

4. Appliqué the scalloped pink solid arch.

5. Use the paper patterns to plan the placement for the flower garden, tracing a few placement lines onto the fabric with the marking pen. Follow the lettering sequence to start. Then appliqué the yellow flowers.

Next appliqué the flower centers, including the turquoise heart. Appliqué the dark green leaves over the yellow print hills, then the blue print flower.

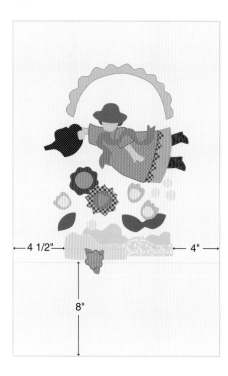

6. Appliqué the left and center rabbits, then the right rabbit. Appliqué the hearts on the rabbits.

Add the Details

Note: Refer to "Embroidery Stitches" on pages 12–13 for stitch diagrams. Refer to the project photo and pattern for placement.

1. Mark the outline of the heart and lettering. With the fabric taped smoothly to a flat surface, paint the heart. Allow the paint to dry thoroughly.
2. Place the yellow arch over the inside edge of the appliquéd pink arch. Using 1 strand of light blue floss, sew running stitches parallel to the edges of the yellow arch. Using 2 strands of light blue floss, buttonhole-stitch the left and center rabbits. Also sew on all of the buttons, referring to the photo on page 106 for placement.
3. Using 2 strands of aqua floss, buttonhole-stitch the scalloped edge of the pink arch. Sew running stitches around the crown of the hat.
4. Using 2 strands of brown floss, stem-stitch the face.
5. Using 2 strands of navy blue floss, backstitch the lettering. Make large French knots on the hat and make small French knots for the rabbits' eyes.
6. Using 2 strands of white floss, satin-stitch the triangle near the spout and backstitch the opening near the handle.
7. Using 2 strands of very light blue floss, buttonhole-stitch the brim of the hat, the sleeve edge, and hem of the dress. Also buttonhole-stitch the edge of the blue print flower.
8. Using 2 strands of orange floss, satin-stitch the shoelaces.
9. Using 2 strands of bright pink floss, chain-stitch the center of the rose/turquoise flower. On the 3 lavender/light blue flowers, satin-stitch across the top of the print pieces. Chain-stitch the flower tendrils. Buttonhole-stitch the edges of the remaining rabbit.
10. Using 2 strands of turquoise floss, chain-stitch the flower stems.

Frame the Design

Note: Refer to "Framing Your Design" on pages 11-12 for general instructions.

Have a professional framer frame the piece, padding the design piece with the fleece.

I Love My Garden Wall Hanging Pattern

Navy blue plaid

Blue print

Turquoise

Orange

Yellow

Green print

Light green

Dark green print

Aqua

Lavender

Rose

Brown

Black print

Yellow print

Tan

Light blue print

Pink floral print

Pink solid

Pink paint

Small pink print

Bright pink print

C

D

I Love My Garden Wall Hanging Pattern

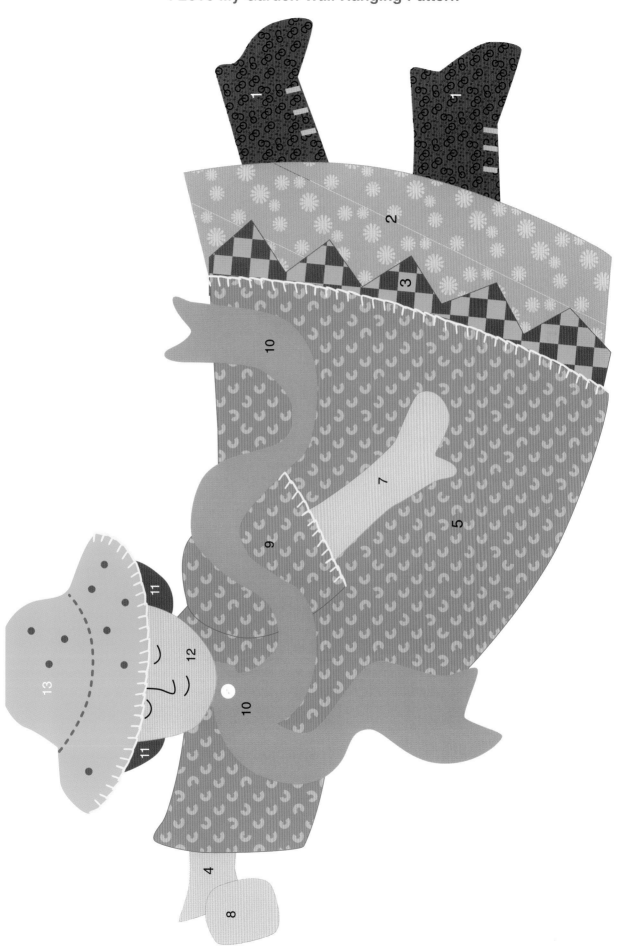

Sow Good Seeds Wall Hanging

Finished Size: 15¼" x 24¼"

Materials

½ yard of 44"-wide blue print for border
¼ yard of 44"-wide gold print for pieced border
¼ yard of 44"-wide cream print for pieced border
11½" x 16½" piece of 44"-wide blue fabric for background
Scraps of cotton fabric in these colors: white, green, light brown, dark brown, gold, pink, light green, green/black print, green print, dark green, blue-green print, rose, medium turquoise, bright turquoise, tan, purple/black print, orange, pale lavender, blue/cream check, and red print
Thread to match fabrics
Large scraps of blue felt
Embroidery floss in these colors: dark brown, light blue, turquoise, green, orange, and gold
½ yard of paper-backed fusible web
23" x 28" piece of polyester fleece
4 brown ⅝"-diameter buttons
Blue permanent fabric pen
Tracing paper and pencil
Air-soluble or water-soluble pen

Appliqué the Design

Note: Refer to "Needle-Turn Appliqué" and "Fusible Appliqué" on pages 8–10 for general instructions. Refer to the project photo and patterns for appliqué placement.

1. Trace the following pattern pieces individually onto the fusible web: banner; house door, window, and path; girl and all clothing; vegetables; and basket. Cut ½" from the drawn lines on the web and fuse to the wrong side of the corresponding fabric scraps.

2. Trace the remaining patterns individually onto tracing paper. Referring to the photo and color key, pin the pattern pieces to the desired fabric and cut them out, adding ¼" seam allowances to all edges. Note that the dashed lines on the pattern indicate where patterns overlap.

3. Following the numerical sequence on the patterns and using needle-turn appliqué, appliqué the white clouds, then the light green treetops to the blue background fabric. Appliqué the tree branches on the left treetop.

4. Appliqué the 2 light green hills. On the right hill, appliqué the gold house, then the dark brown roof.

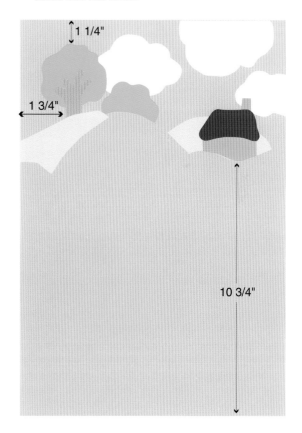

5. Working from top to bottom, layer and appliqué the remaining hills. The finished background should measure 11½" x 16½".

6. Cut out the fabric pieces for the door, window, and path. Peel off the paper backing and place the pieces fusible side down on the background, using the photo as a guide. Fuse in place.

7. Cut out and fuse the pink banner above and to the left of the house.

8. Cut out and fuse the carrot, then the 2 tomatoes to the blue felt. Fuse the blue/cream check basket onto the blue felt; set aside.

9. Cut out and fuse the girl's boots to the blue felt, then the right hand. Fuse the right sleeve, the dress, then the bright turquoise scarf. Next, fuse the left hand, then the remaining sleeve. Fuse the face, hair, and then the hat.

10. Cut the basket and girl out of the felt, trimming a scant ⅛" outside the designs. Appliqué to the background.

11. Cut out and fuse the remaining 3 carrots and the 5 lavender vegetables in place.

Embroider the Details

Note: Refer to "Embroidery Stitches" on pages 12–13 for stitch diagrams. Refer to the project photo and pattern for placement.

1. Using 2 strands of light blue floss, make 5 French knots on the hill below the house. Sew running stitches around the brim of the hat. Backstitch the folds at the hem of the dress. Sew a V at the top of each tomato. Also tack-stitch around each lavender vegetable.

2. Using 2 strands of orange floss, tack-stitch the edges of the carrots.

3. Using 2 strands of green floss, stem-stitch the carrot tops. Sew a V in the lavender vegetable tops.

4. Using 2 strands of dark brown floss, embroider the eyes, nose, and mouth.

5. Using 2 strands of turquoise floss, stitch diagonal lines of long running stitches on the dress.

6. Using 2 strands of gold floss, sew diagonal lines of running stitches on the blue-green print hill.

Finish the Background

1. From the cream and gold prints, cut 2 strips, each 1½"-wide. Place one of each print right sides together, and stitch on the long edge with a ¼" seam allowance. Repeat. Cut the strips into 1½" segments; you will need 62 segments.

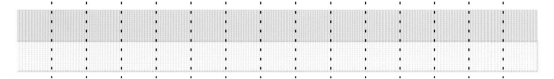

2. Stitch the segments together, alternating fabrics, to make the following checkerboard pieces: 2 units of 2 x 15 blocks and 2 units of 2 x 16 blocks.

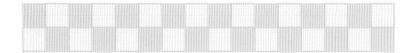

3. Stitch the longer checkerboard strips to the sides of the background, aligning the top and bottom edges. Stitch the shorter checkerboard strips to the top and bottom edges, maintaining the checkerboard pattern in the corners.
4. From the blue print, cut 2 strips, each 4" x 21½", and 2 strips, each 4" x 15½". Stitch the shorter strips to the top and bottom of the checkerboard, aligning the edges. Stitch the longer strips to the sides.

Finish the Design

Note: Refer to "Framing Your Design" on pages 11–12 for general instructions

1. Using the blue fabric pen, print "Sow Good Seeds" on the pink banner.
2. Sew a button at each corner of the appliquéd center.
3. Have a professional framer frame the piece, padding it with the fleece.

Sow Good Seeds Wall Hanging Pattern

- White
- Green
- Light brown
- Dark brown
- Gold
- Pink
- Light green
- Green/Black print
- Green print
- Dark green
- Blue-green print
- Rose
- Bright turquoise
- Medium turquoise
- Tan
- Purple/Black print
- Orange
- Pale lavender
- Blue/Cream check
- Red print

10

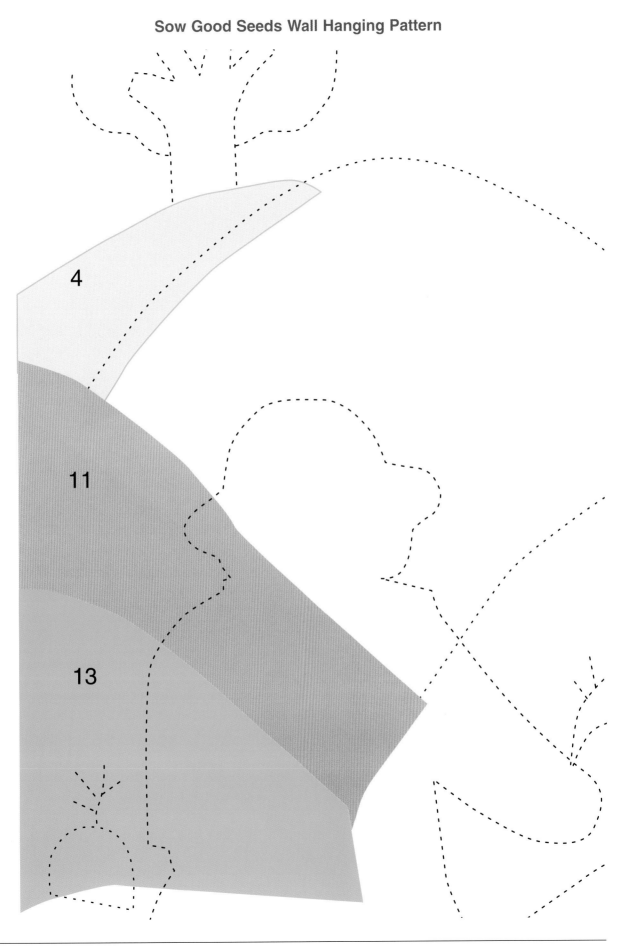

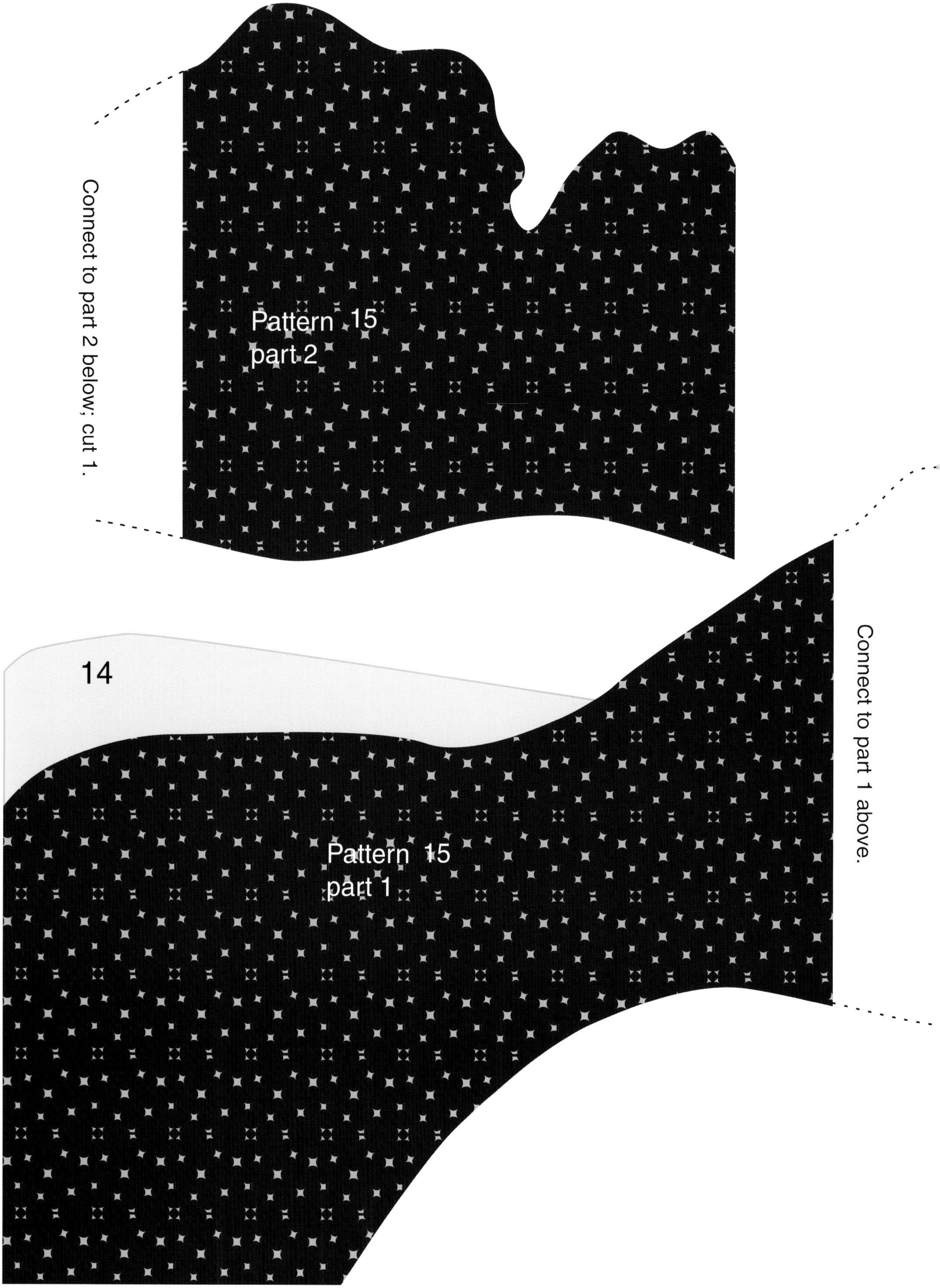

Connect to part 2 below; cut 1.

Pattern 15
part 2

14

Pattern 15
part 1

Connect to part 1 above.

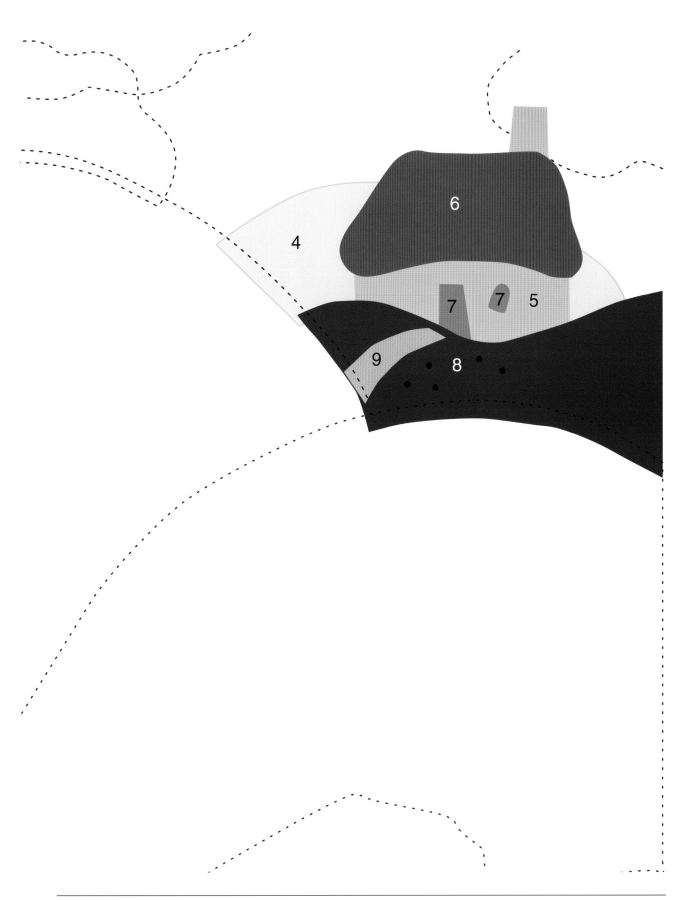

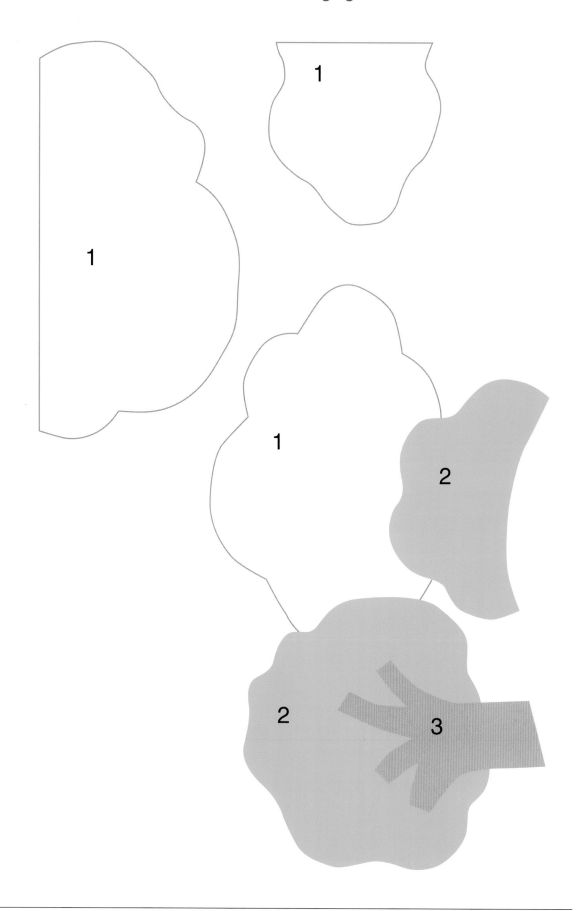

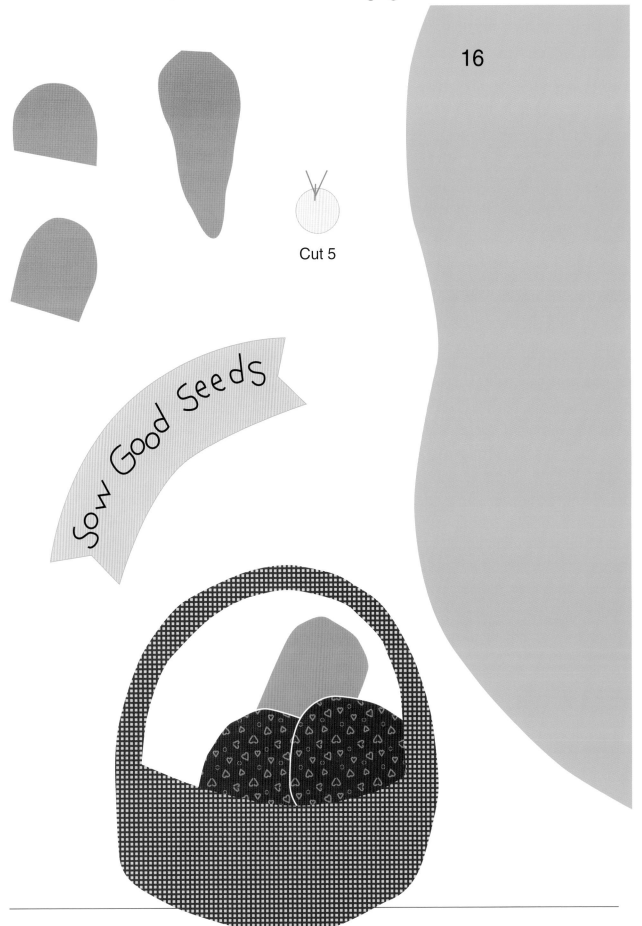

16

Cut 5

Sow Good Seeds

About the Authors

With more than thirty-five years of design experience to their credit, Trice Boerens and Terrece Beesley have designed for Better Homes and Gardens, Oxmoor House, Leisure Arts, the American School of Needlework, Woman's *Day*, and Coats and Clark.

Trice is well known for her contemporary twists on traditional quiltmaking designs. She works in numerous artistic mediums, including quilting, watercolor, wood, and printmaking. Terrece co-founded the Vanessa-Ann Collection, a leading company in the needlework and craft industry for many years. More than one-hundred publications showcase her design talents.